D1476323

SIX

SIX

poems

Julie Marie Wade

Red Hen Press | *Pasadena, CA*

SIX

Copyright © 2016 by Julie Marie Wade

All Rights Reserved

No part of this book may be used or reproduced in any manner whatsoever without the prior written permission of both the publisher and the copyright owner.

Book layout by Pricilla Delatorre

Library of Congress Cataloging-in-Publication Data

Names: Wade, Julie Marie, author.
Title: Six : poems / Julie Marie Wade.
Description: First edition. | Pasadena, CA : Red Hen Press, [2016]
Identifiers: LCCN 2016023199 | ISBN 9781597097215 (softcover : acid-free
   paper) | ISBN 9781597095051 (ebook)
Classification: LCC PS3623.A345 A6 2016 | DDC 811/.6—dc23
LC record available at https://lccn.loc.gov/2016023199

The publication of this book was made possible by A Room of Her Own Foundation's To the Lighthouse Poetry Publication Prize, awarded in 2014 for the best unpublished poetry collection by a woman.

The National Endowment for the Arts, the Los Angeles County Arts Commission, the Los Angeles Department of Cultural Affairs, the Dwight Stuart Youth Fund, the Pasadena Arts & Culture Commission and the City of Pasadena Cultural Affairs Division, the Ahmanson Foundation, and Sony Pictures Entertainment partially support Red Hen Press.

First Edition
Published by Red Hen Press
www.redhen.org

For Angie

I thought of you. Whom I love, madly.

CONTENTS

FOREWORD

I chose *SIX* not in spite of but because of its discursiveness, its willingness to wander through the poem with technique at hand, but also a permit to allow both substantive and ephemeral material to wander into the field of the poem and exit without a conclusive goal in mind. It's an accumulative project, inclusive, and busy about the business of sifting and sorting through this thing we call life that we carry out in this creation we call a body on this tumultuous blue orb we call earth.

—C.D. Wright

The sun rises without me
The moon has no thought of me
The crow & the swallow have something else to say

There's always another side to things, & another side,
A glass like the house of language,
A glass—
Though whether cracked or sure or penetrable
I did not say.

—Suzanne Paola

LATCHKEY

Anything—by these terms—may be a poem.

How does that feel?

Cold . . . *as a stethoscope . . . as a dense fog . . .*

Does a poem know its own name?

Will it come when called?

Will it come if you call it something different?

Today a truck parked in a tunnel proclaimed to me:

"Trucks are like women—if it's not yours, don't touch it."

I'm over-punctuating: there was no comma, no long dash—surely no "quotation marks."

The truck, stagnant & driverless, interrupted my train of thought,

firing—or so it seemed—a live assault.

"When the times get tough, the tough get going"—

And the weak intellectualize

That's what I thought anyway—   weak & voiceless in a tunnel
                    hollow as my pagan heart.

(Do you like that flourish? That flare of melodrama?
When I send a signal, I'm seldom subtle.
I call six times just to be sure you heard.)

First, I laughed because it lets the sting out. Laughter deflates the ripe balloon.

Then, I squirreled around the subject & made a strike through on the words inside my mind.

    Improper syntax

    Revise!

    Suggest alternatives:

(*singular*) "A truck is like a woman: if it's not yours, don't touch it."

    Aphoristic. Expanded simile. A recognizable rhetorical form à la Eleanor Roosevelt,

    sometimes credited to Nancy Reagan—*& who to believe?*

            "A woman is like a tea bag: you never know how strong she is
                until she gets into hot water."

And that's another thing: the problem of "it" & of pronouns all together

A tea bag is now a "she"   (personification?) (anthropomorphism?) (pathetic fallacy?)

A woman is now an "it"

Comparing animate to inanimate is risky business.

Risky Business. 1983 Tom Cruise flick where he dances in his underwear. *Beware*: may not be appropriate for all audiences.

(*plural*) "Trucks are like women: if they're not yours, don't touch them."

That solves the problem of parallel structure, of noun-verb agreement, of contradictory pronouns.

But every statement poses problems the words can't discern, those heel-nippers:

Ideology   &   *Context*

I think a poem is a thought.

(*Is the converse true? Is a thought a poem?*)

The statement a dart, the mind a board.

Questions raised by the assertion—this bumper sticker, this city slicker's fortune cookie.

Two-for-one special at the cinema:

City Slickers (plural, non-possessive). 1991. Billy Crystal in mid-life crisis. [followed by]

Fortune Cookie. 1999. "Three couples, one night—No two fortunes are ever the same." [not to be confused with]
The Wrong Fortune Cookie. 2002. "Because some cookies just don't have the right answers."
And there's another one, from 1966, with Goldie Hawn.

There is no evidence to suggest that women & trucks have anything in common. Some women drive trucks. Some men drive women crazy. I was almost driven crazy by a man—not that I blame him entirely, since "crazy" is a lazy word & quite subjective, a bead on a sliding scale. Let's just say I couldn't stand the sound of him crushing cans of Barq's root beer between his bare hands & tossing them across the floor, like a new sport: a combination baseball/bowling.

I think a poem is a thought.

Linda B. used to say, before she married Paul A. & became a different person:

"If you love him, you won't mind the little things he does. If he throws his socks on the floor, or his underwear, you'll just pick them up & toss them in the wash. After a while, you won't

even notice
anymore."

I think a poem is a thought *&* a disruption of thought.

Jeanette Winterson on Virginia Woolf: "She was an experimenter who managed to combine the pleasure of narrative with those forceful interruptions the mind needs to wake itself."

Wake   or   *rouse.*

I had not been sleeping, not like the Beauty whose pointer was poised, then pierced on a spinning wheel, drowsing under the weight of that spell.

—As under glass. An artifact of difference for the masculine museum.

—As pheasant even. The elegant. The hunted. The contained.

I had not been asked to turn flax into gold.

Yet how that *permission* (birthright?) (compulsion?) binds like a contract I was coerced to sign!

Passive	I do
Kempt	I do
Inured	I most certainly do

> (And what is this word but a 'j' away from *injured*)

"You're such a spitfire!" my father exclaimed, but neither he nor I were sure what this should mean.

> *Spitfire*, as in *The Spitfire Grill*: "To a town with no future comes a girl with a past." 1996. 3 nominations, 1 win.
>
> As in, literally: "capable of spitting fire."

We have a dictionary in our house now. I can look things up. Like raising a periscope over a very high (*Secret Garden* high) wall:

spit·fire *n.* a quick-tempered or highly excitable person [then the subordinate clause],
    especially a girl or woman.

If I were Gretel (or Hansel maybe), what kind of seeds would I throw down?
(Not *crumbs*, you see, which decompose—but seeds: resolutions: the kinds of things that grow)

Flax, Sesame, Poppy

And from flax shall come doubloons a' plenty

And from sesame shall come streets paved with gold

And from poppy—sweet poppy—a field of flowers & a deep dream like an after-thought

I think a poem is pre-meditated. Like a crime. Like the hardest kind of crime to solve.

If I were Hansel (or Gretel maybe), what kind of stalk, what kind of story?

Experiment, Pleasure, Interruption

—the spitfire

—the extortionist

—the "break in the flow"

I think a poem is a thought. And a counter-thought. A promise & its palinode.

Where the pretty words kiss & crumble—*flummox & fawn—*

Where
        "visceral whiplash,"

                "cerebral serenade,"

                                        the pressure to combine these pleasures . . .

Anything may be a poem.

Is there a "theme"? Is there a "thesis"? Is there a "point"?

You say: "Maybe you're looking at this the wrong way."

(A shrug.) (An eyebrow raise.)

"Maybe that truck wasn't talking to you. Maybe you intercepted someone else's message."

If the words are little inkblots, like I like to believe,
then we learn to have a sixth sense about them:

> *The Sixth Sense.* 1999 drama about a boy who communicates with
> people who don't know they're dead. "Not every gift is a blessing."

Like if I say *story*, you don't have to say *moral*, even if it's the first word that comes to mind.

Or maybe you do, & that's good too because then we can talk about it: this assumption that morals underlie
things—undergird them: that old graffiti beneath the green bridge.

Or if you say *poem*, & I say *malice*, to throw you off, but also because I think a poem has a dark side.

> *Malice.* 1993. Baldwin. Pullman. Kidman. "You ask me if I have a
> God complex. Let me tell you something: I *am* God."

Poet.

Now there's one with a *God Complex.*

- No, I don't think poets are "more spiritual than other people."

- No, I don't think it's a "gift" or a "blessing."

- Yes, I think it's "work."

- Yes, I think it's a "worthwhile undertaking."

How come, if I tell a joke, no one calls me a *comedian*?
But I write a poem, & just like that, I'm a *poet*.

(A shrug.) (An eyebrow raise.)

Earl Lovelace used to ask, rum-soused & wide-eyed:
"Where is the story?"

Only he stretched *story* out to three syllables & let it linger like taste on tongue . . .

Where   is   the   st   oo   ry?

As if the story were hiding somewhere, that tiresome imp.
That cow that jumped over the moon.

I have been accused of being cold.

—*as a stethoscope*

—*as a dense fog*

My gears & wires, like a yellowed slip, have been accused of showing.

What ever happened to Show-and-Tell? Nowadays everyone wants a Confession.

con·fes·sion *n.* avowal of faith (or) admission of guilt.

A promise & its palinode.

Sharon Olds on brainpower: "To me, the mind seems to be spread out in the whole body."

I can *show* you what I see, I can *tell* you what I think, but do I owe you my faith or my guilt?

Terry Crabtree in *Wonder Boys*: "What he means is . . . it's difficult to distill the essence of a book because it lives in the mind."

And where is the mind again?

All over the body.

My Dear Mr. Descartes, we've come full circle   *& still no sign of the Soul*

Here about the time, counter & clockwise & running out of & once upon, I was a citizen of a strange land of phrases. Province of "white elephants" & "elbow grease." No table quite complete without a "cheese ball." And my father called his suitcase a "grip" & gripped it tighter, not sure who would be first to fall. And my mother, who was once almost eaten by a mountain lion, survived to play dice games like "Fill or Bust" & piano instead of accordion.

And so in this way, I learned there are rooms inside words, spaces for a mind to crouch inside them.

Crouching Tiger, Hidden Dragon. 2000 Ang Lee film
about a stolen sword & a notorious fugitive.

("About": that endless handkerchief a magician pulls from his pocket.)

Who hasn't written the poem she's supposed to write?
The teachers will praise you for it. The class will agree.
There will be a lot of buzz about "accessibility."

How does that feel?

I never saw *Dead Poets Society*—or once, with a fever, in a college dorm. I kissed my boyfriend afterward.
He was churchy & prim & pleased with himself. The next day he started "coming down with something."

A whole architecture rests on a single word:

coming down   (or)   *letting*   (or)   *going*

He did the second but never the third . . .

Or when my grandmother, rattled or pleased, exhales an "Oh my word!"

—As if she couldn't pick one

—As if I could ever blame her

I think a poem is a thought. I think a word is a room.

Words in a poem are optional.
(See *Moonlight & Valentino*. 1995. Elizabeth Perkins & Whoopi Goldberg.)

Have you ever spun doughnuts in a parking lot?
Popped wheelies?
Gone for a bumper ski?

The sheer futility . . . *of actions unprovoked . . . of outcomes unexpected*

But you like it: Sisyphus meets Hercules on the rope tow to the future & the present (for once) is

neither a

gift

nor a

blessing.

The Gift: 2000 Sam Raimi thriller starring Cate Blanchett:
"The only witness to the crime was not even there."

Questions raised by the assertion—*how much of the poem is futile? how much inevitable?*

ad hoc *adj.* for the special purpose or end at hand & for no other; also, by extension, improvised or impromptu; as in "case-by-case basis."

post hoc *adj.* the logical fallacy of believing that temporal succession implies a causal relation; in or of the form of argument in which one event is asserted to be the cause of a later event simply by virtue of having happened earlier; as in "post hoc reasoning."

And what to believe?

Kierkegaard on progress: "One must live life forwards, though understand it backwards."

This the problem of the post hoc, the poem's problem, Houdini's chained box submerged in water, yet the contents disappear . . . or were they ever really there to begin with?

Does reflection generate insight or delusion?

Is hindsight 20/20 or profoundly blind?

In my life as an amanuensis, I have typed these words, fingers haltingly across the keys, that fragile feeling rising up in my mouth & pressing deep into the soft palate tissue: *The type of "understanding" he cites is that found in everyday life; we begin with what happened (consequences) & find appropriate causes (antecedents), often by creating a "good story"—i.e., one compatible with our own & our culture's understanding of life.*

In love with a woman, the oxytocin overdrive:

My mother first, sobbing into the phone: "So that's why you don't wear make-up."

And then my father: "She was always different. Not that she played with G.I. Joes, but she didn't seem to like those Barbies either."

I think a poem is the best story we have.

(Remember when "telling stories" was the same as "telling lies"?)

Rapunzel releases her long braid.
Material she has made useful.
A transformation: this yellow ladder of hair.

Wait for it—*the crux, the fulcrum*.

Somewhere the poem starts to reveal intention. A rope dangles from a tower window.

(Will you climb it?
Will it hold you?
Will something in you have to give way?)

If I say *story*, you don't have to say *lie*, even if it's the first word that comes to mind.

Maybe you say *myth*—a lie cloaked in cache—or *superstition*, post hoc caveat.

Or if you say *poem*, & I say *comeuppance* or *closed system* or *schadenfreude*—
my fondness for compound words; a house with an attic inside.

I think the poem is an alter-ego.

Not an after-school special or a tinder box.

(Where the thesis, also the anti-thesis . . .)

Not only to educate—
Not just to contain—

Think about the "a" that makes *person* a *persona*.

Think about the shape of those words.

Like if I tried to draw a line between James Stewart & George Bailey—
right down the middle of their bodies.

(The same body, but not the same mind . . .)

I think a poem is a thought with a transom. I think a word is a room with a skylight.

Crawl spaces.

Curtains.

Or my aunt:

how she could never look at Bing Crosby the same way again: now knowing

he had beat his kids & been a Catholic.

The man who was my grandma's window-washer for close to twenty years, confiding:

"I washed windows for Donna Reed. You never met a nicer lady. *Real* sincere.
She didn't play no *character* on television. She was just bein' herself."

Does it stay separate?   I wonder.
Like the *poet* & *speaker*,   the *actor* & *part*?

One a dart, the other a board.

Or the *woman* who is also a *wife*—her name she has changed to duplicate her husband's.

Coordinate.

Copy.

What of the *maiden* name & the *married* name?

Mary Hatch, then two words, *poof!* She's *Mary Bailey*

It's a Wonderful Life: Frank Capra's 1946 classic about a
disheartened businessman who is given a chance to see "what the world
would be like without" him. A horror film. A promise—& its palinode.

From which: a new word:

Cap·ra·esque *adj.* of or evocative of the movies of Frank Capra, often promoting the positive social

effects of individual acts of courage.
And the best piece of advice I ever took from a film: "Why don't you kiss her instead of talking her to death?"

Like a trap door & falling through it, or Alice down the rabbit hole, or Dorothy caught out wandering in a storm.

Something there is that doesn't love a wall—but wants it all the same.

- No, I'm not trying to "exclude" you

- No, I wouldn't say I tend to "dissociate"

- Yes, I will leave a light on for you

- Yes, I will place a key under the mat

I think a poem is a thought.
A three-story stand-alone with an alley out back.
A long braid. A wrench & a rope.

No pasting Zuzu's petals back.

                                        (Though we love them: *these beautiful lies*)

Not *happily* always,

                                        But   *alert* &   *ever mindful*   after.

I think a poem is a thought & a compendium of thoughts.
A skeletal probe & a white-water raft.

Also (clearly):   a metaphor.

Also (necessarily):   an inventory.
Remove stars from eyes √

Repeat maxim: *Good fences make good neighbors* √

Lock back door √

Lock front door √

Open shutters on upstairs windows √

Shovel walks √

Warm engine √

Leave a light on √

Place key (*duplication prohibited*) under the dark-woven mat √

LAYOVER

And what would you call this?

I need the *right* word,   word for

"space."

Roget's, my language bandit, my loquacious

partner in rhyme:

space/place
location/distanciation

interstice
caesura
gap
(w)hole
open
empty
prairie
possible

ℓℓℓℓℓℓℓℓℓℓℓℓℓℓℓℓℓℓℓℓℓℓℓℓℓℓℓℓQAAAAAAAAAAAAAAAAAAAAAAAAA

Now space is different in the airport.

There is an "outer" & an "inner," one cosmos that can't be reached

     without a ticket.

Please . . .   *remove your shoes . . .*

I am especially interested in the

"amnesty box."

Discard anonymously any weapons—or items that might be used as weapons—& no harm will befall you.

Something like that.
I tend to jazz things up.
My paraphrases are always prolific.

Have you noticed how the night sky is strangely dimmer

    than it was when you were a child?

                                  We need more stars,

                    & not just as punctuation marks or dotting "i"s

        With a Southern accent, *eyes* & *ice* are easily confused (I've listened)

Both can be cold—& melting.

topography *n.* **1a** a detailed description, representation on a map, etc., of the natural & artificial features of a town, district, etc. **b** such features. **2** *Anat.* the mapping of the surface of the body with reference to the parts beneath.

Outside the neighbors are having a picnic. The father kneels at his Hibachi, the mother smokes Marlboros & braids her daughters' hair.

They don't know it yet (nor will they ever), but their presence is crucial to this poem.

I have just returned from the airport. I am hungry. What they are having looks good.

The mother glances up at my window. Sees me scrubbing the plates I meant to wash days ago. Residue of old meals: spaghetti sauce, oats with brown sugar.

The mother glances up at my window & feels sorry for me. Thinks I am lonely. Imagines I live here alone.

Topos, a place, a common place.

We used to sit for hours watching the planes. Imagining the luxury of travel.

In an airport, you could say anything. It wasn't dangerous. Strangers understood the *now or never.*

topology *n. Math.* the study of geometrical properties & spatial relations unaffected by the continuous change of shape or size of figures.

As if the poem must be a proof of something. As if it must begin with a given.

Two truths: a *been* & a *going.*

We need more words, more stars . . .

If I wasn't really here, how could it hurt so much to think about leaving?

We are almost out of potatoes . . .

Does the chimney get lonely in summertime?

Outside the neighbors are having a picnic. The father drapes tinsel over a section of cyclone fence. The mother rocks the low-birthweight baby.

I have judged them. Without meaning to. I have judged them from my kitchen window.

In Atlanta, my lover's plane is landing. No good word for this. For *lover*.

toponym *n*. **1** a place-name. **2** a descriptive place-name, usu. derived from a topographical feature of the place.

Always an "outer" & an "inner."

If we know this much, why not more? Why (still) the jet-lag of the senses?

Outside the father hugs his second daughter. It is her birthday. She has candles & a cake with cream cheese frosting like the ones my mother used to make.

cake/make/bake/take/shake/stake

Always an "outer" & an "inner." Always something "at stake."

If you were here, we would watch vampire movies.

Kiss each other—   not in the kitchen.

The neighbors, you say,   *the neighbors are watching.*

Two truths: a *been* & a *going.*

Your sister lives in a big, rich house. She is younger than you are. A pilot's wife.

Why are there words for this—for *sibling*, for *spouse*?

                                        Has the language not learned us yet?

toponomy *n.* the study of the place-names of a region.

>   *partner*
>   *companion*
>   *cohabitant*
>   *friend*
>   *special friend*
>   *life-mate*
>   *room-mate*
>   *consort*
>   *significant other*

When I say them, when I am spoken about, I feel the space (absence) (wound) left by their sound.

The illegitimate language:

            "Do you mean your *business* partner?"

            "Chess?" "Golf?" "Running?"

"*Who now?*"

"Surely not *sexual*—you don't mean—"

"*Who?*"

"Is there a second bedroom?"

"Just sharing expenses till the right men come along . . ."

"The other one: what was her name?"

I am lonely

      as a chimney

            in summertime.

Outside the neighbors do not live in a big, rich house. They are younger than we are. Maybe the same age.

Outside I remember the neighbors last summer. He with his loud temper, she with her belly swollen large. The children without their shirts on. The turtle they captured & kept in the pool.

If a poem has *givens*, what are the *takens*? What does it mean that something has *taken place*?

    Like stealing second base?

    We don't have bases in our ballgame.

    Your mother, hypothetically speaking: "Gay men I can understand. But women just don't *fit* together."

Always an "outer" & an "inner."

The chimney—& the smoke.

Topos, a place, a common place.

The problem with the past is everyone remembers it differently.

I'm afraid life accumulates like the body count.

One cosmos that can't be reached without a ticket.

    Jimmy Stewart

    Princess Diana

    Mother Teresa

    Gwendolyn Brooks

    Robert Creeley

    Pope John Paul II

Does it matter that no one understands who we are?

Not even the neighbors. Especially (not even) the neighbors.

In Atlanta, my lover & her sister follow the moving sidewalk. They are *family*. This we have a word for.

(kith &) kin, kinsmen, kindred, kinfolk, kinsfolk, next of kin, relatives, relations, folks, people, one's own flesh & blood, one's nearest & dearest, household, ménage, children, offspring, progeny, ancestors, forebears, forefathers, progenitors, ancestry, parentage, descent, derivation, lineage, pedigree, genealogy, house, bloodline, dynasty, stock, strain

Outside the neighbors are having a birthday party for their second daughter. She is young. Three or four.

They are young, a young couple, a husband & wife with children.

I feel old like a chimney, lonely. I would smoke too if I hadn't given it up

orphan *n. & v.* **1** a child bereaved of a parent or usu. both parents. **2** a young animal that has lost its mother. **3** a person or thing bereft of previous protection, support, advantages.

Airports make orphans of us all.

The heavy baggage, & no one to help you lift it. Looking for someone you won't find. Claims. Tickets. Gates. Crowd. Delayed arrival. Early departure. *Can they do that?* Stubs for a scrapbook. If you save that sort of thing.

Please . . .   remove your shoes . . .

Outside the neighbors have prepared a picnic dinner. They are a *family*, brittle & belonging. Like the morning when, in the early heat, he filled the children's pool with cool water from the hose. She came outside. Her feet were swollen. I was in the kitchen making coffee. My Love asleep. My *beloved*. Do you like that word any better? It's what Helen Hunt said at the Oscars. Her beloved was a man. They aren't together anymore. It unraveled. I'm not sure how this happens, only that it does. I was once beloved of a man. You live your days answering to names you don't believe in. Altars are for alterations. I could never be "cut from the same cloth" as my parents. And look at me now, a chimney of cracked brick, sloppy mortar. I wouldn't change a thing. I want you here & now so much . . . The silence is killing me. The little girls are laughing with their light blond hair. I'm afraid to say hello to the mother, afraid of what she will say once she understands how you are not just my "room-mate," not just, as my mother called you, "the meter maid."

euphemism *n.* **1** a mild or vague expression substituted for one thought to be too harsh or direct (e.g., *pass over* for *die*). **2** the use of such expressions.

I have a passport with only one stamp.

Erma Bombeck was my mother's favorite. Erma Bombeck said, "When you look like your passport photo it's time to go home."

I don't know where that is now.

Two truths: a *been* & a *going*.

Do you see the problem, the necessity of "space"?

middle ground
ground cover
nuances
nicotine
nepotism
not without a _____

Fill in your own blanks

ticket
cosmos
weapon

Items that might be used as weapons

paperclip
matchbook

dictionary-&-thesaurus

I am especially interested in the

"amnesty box."

Your parents have driven down to Atlanta for the weekend. Somewhere outside Peach Tree City your mother tears the map. A plain-faced man in a golf cart breaks down by the side of the road.

Automobiles are optional in Peach Tree City. A good golf cart is essential.

The neighbors, Mr. & Mrs. Too Many Children, suffer from too little space. She fills up the pool with her body. Legs swollen. Fingers too. He massages her shoulders. *Maybe he loves her.* I pour coffee into steaming cups. *Maybe they wanted this baby.* I carry them upstairs to our *topos*, our common place.

Is there a "given," for any of us?
I am a poet, not a mathematician.
I want to give you something I cannot take back.

My parents, in a certain sense, have *passed over*. In the airport sense, our affections were *terminal*.

origin *n.* **1** a beginning or starting point; a derivation; a source. **2** a person's ancestry. **3** *Anat.* **a** a place at which a muscle is firmly attached. **b** a place where a nerve or blood vessel begins or branches from a main nerve or blood vessel. **4** *Math.* a fixed point from which coordinates are measured.

Tonight the darkness languishes (languages).

Outside the neighbors are blowing out candles & switching on lights. The party is over.

Tonight a pilot steers his aircraft into the hangar. Is that what it's called—*a hanger?* He is driving home on a steel highway to his wife & his wife's family, who are called *in-laws*. See, there is a name for this. And the lights have gone out in Georgia, for a while.

Another night this would have been another poem. Maybe cheerier, or maybe (it's possible) more somber. But the point is . . . *fixed*. The moment . . . *mandatory*. And when I *pass over*, as we all must, I want to pass over *trying*.

I have icy eyes in the steel dark. They are cold—& melting.

I miss my mother.
(no)
I miss wishing for the mother I wish I had.

I miss my lover.
(no)
I miss wishing for the word for what we have.

I glance out my window at the mother. Watch her emptying the ice trays & folding the tablecloth. Think *yes, it is hard work you're doing*. Think *no, I don't begrudge you your labor*.

I glance out my window at the mother. I have stopped feeling sorry for her. I have stopped imagining her misery & ceased discounting her joy.

ℓℓℓℓℓℓℓℓℓℓℓℓℓℓℓℓℓℓℓℓℓℓℓℓℓℓℓℓℓℓℓℓℓAAAAAAAAAAAAAAAAAAAAAAAAAAAA

original *adj. & n.* **1** existing from the beginning; innate. **2** novel; inventive; creative. **3** serving as a pattern; not derivative or imitative; firsthand.

Have you noticed how the night sky is strangely dimmer

      than it was when you were a child?

We need more stars.

If I knew the words, I would meet the mother at the fence that divides our territories, meet her with the three children in tow (two little girls asleep in their dresses, a boy-baby pressed to her chest).

I would say, "I don't understand your world—how it works, how it breaks, how it heals."

Discard anonymously any weapons

I would say, "It's good to meet you. I hope you're happy with the family that you have."

Or items that might be used as weapons

I would say, "There's someone I love living with me in this house, & when she returns, I'd like you to meet her."

And no harm will befall you.

MAIDENHEAD

It all begins with Red. She was a good girl, couldn't have been more than twelve or thirteen, nothing on her mind but an innocent visit to Grandmother's house. Problem with the child isn't that she's vain but that she's vulnerable—or so the story instructs us to believe. She has a showy red cape & a pretty red mouth & legs growing longer by the hour. She isn't afraid of her body, like they tell us in books. She likes it: little sounds it makes, way it bends into the wind & curls up on the bed & climbs things, straddles them. She thinks to herself, *I'm part boy & part cat, I can do anything*, & thinking this way, she can. One of the things Red does best is playing hard-to-get. She likes keep-away, too: all that jazz. So it occurs to me that the wolf might not be your ordinary, run-of-the-mill, woodsy-type predator. Rather, he might stand in for a certain shy lad out to take his revenge. "You broke my heart!" he howls at the midday sun, muted enough to resemble a moon. She takes the locket he gave her—gold, with a picture inside—& grinds it to dust under the point of her shoe. "No," she says, curling her lip, "*now* I've broken your heart."

Somewhere in Nashville tonight

     some two   are about to be

                sorely

                      disappointed

Same is true of Cincinnati, Cleveland.

Pittsburgh even: largest city in Appalachia—

> where the Monongahela & the Allegheny

> (& a few furtive lovers)   awkwardly unite

Sure, you've heard about gettin' lucky in Kentucky, you've heard Virginia is for lovers, you've heard

> But you ain't *seen* nothin' yet.

I was supposed to be guarding it.

> *Vigilant.* Watchtowers, crows' nests. A pair of PermaFocus Free Wide Angle binoculars.

I was supposed to sound the alarm at any sign of intrusion.

> *Kicking & screaming.* Movie theatres, parking lots. A Z-force 300,000 volt stun gun.

"What is it?"
> "What is what?"

"The *it*. The *treasure*."
> "Why, your most precious gift, you silly goose—the irreplaceable gift of your *girlhood*."

I heard *hood*, & I wanted it—*oh how I wanted it*—that elegant, velveteen cowl.
Scarlet. Turquoise. Chartreuse. Salmon. (Best crayons of the 64-piece set.)

Or that deep ecclesiastical Purple,
> like cloth draped over the cross at Lenten service.

"When can I have it?"
> "What?"

"My girl hood. Is it coming by post? Will I have to sign?"
> "But darling, you've always had it. You're born with it."

"What do you mean?"

"It's *innate*."

Like *ornate*, a word I knew better.

> This body of mine: pert & new & green as a Christmas tree: gangly.
> But what of the ornaments—garland & tinsel? jingling bells? Where does this girl hood *go*?

Dot has a dilemma. She keeps meeting the wrong kind of men: no-brainers, barbarians, buffoons. Whole series of tedious encounters. Her pleasure-quest culminates in an opium den. *What would Joycelyn Elders do?* she wonders, wading through the rainbow-floral haze. There was a special on cable just before the cyclone struck. If only she had ordered the Sue Johanson Royal Wizard for $49.95 plus tax (S & H not included). It would be here by now, here in her hot little hand. *If only.* But the drag queen in the pink gown & glittering crown knows better, suggests the essential accoutrement has been with her all along. *Pay no attention to the men behind the curtain*, to the misfits you've harbored between your emerald sheets. "Close your eyes, darling. Clear your mind. Tap your euphemism at least three times." Waving her Hitachi Wand & smiling grandly. New basket sticker for a hot air balloon: floating away, *Magic Happens*. "Repeat as needed. The power is yours. Be happy, my dear, ever after."

Somewhere in the Smoky Mountains—

> Or the San Fernando Valley—

Or the Grand Teton Wildlife Preserve—

> > He in black, She in white, world between them
> > sedimentary gray

How not to be hoodwinked into believing this life better than the last:

> chance meeting, changed name, close quarters on the honeymoon cruise . . .

The little snickers, the faux blush
Her mother's friend who wrapped a shiny box of air:

Wear <u>this</u> on your wedding night, & everything will be all right

All that close scrutiny, all those danders up
White lace garter pinching at her thigh
Bouquet tossed strategically away

There was once a raven-haired woman—young but wise—old enough at least to know better.
Night before the ceremony, she broke into a flush, which on closer inspection
revealed a wicked case of hives. Whole body blistered red, emergency room for a
swollen tongue, her breath choked in: quick gasps, hasty swallows. And the doctor said,
"You might want to re-think this thing," or something to that effect, but she was stubborn
(more stubborn than she was wise), & so she married him the next morning, patchy skin
concealed beneath her requisite white. Did they ever talk about it? Did he touch the places her
body had (strategically) rejected him? Seven months later, they parted ways. She bit her tongue
then, clamped it tight. All the things she could have said but chose—stubbornly—not to say.

I was the only child: my mother's daughter, my father's son:

    Whosoever thou needest me to be

It was unclear from the beginning, however, to whom my body belonged.

    Did they own that also? Was there a mortgage coming due?

                  And who *were* these people really?

  Strangers . . . the only strangers I happened to know.

               Miss   Mrs.   Ms.   Mr.

                  (circle one)

"What she really needs is a good roll in the hay."

"Who?"

  "No one."

"What does that mean?"

  "Will you give us a minute please?"

"Why?"

  "Outside. Now."

The Strangers are talking:

    He in soft tones, She in harsher   (worlds between us, walls)

What I know about hay amounts to very little. I know it can give you "fever" in the springtime, fresh pollen-clouds rising from my mother's flowers. I know it is sometimes gathered & rolled—*is that what they meant?*—into bales, which we see as we drive down the Oregon coast on our way to summer vacation. But when I look up "bale" in my desktop *Merriam-Webster* dictionary, I learn it is a noun meaning first, "great evil," & second, "woe or sorrow." These definitions trouble me, turning suddenly sinister those wide curious carpets of cut grass cured for fodder.

And what about hay*rides* & hay*stacks*—that miraculous rock formation off the coast of Cannon Beach? Were those *evil* too? Was there something *sorrowful* lurking in the inter-tide, pooled among the chitons & starfish & fuchsia-bright sea anemones?

     This *That* *The Other* *All of the Above*

       (circle one)

"Time to hit the hay," my parents chime,

  And my bottom lip trembles a little.

    I bite my tongue then, clamp it tight.

The next morning I summon my courage & ask:

    "Why is the Needle in the Haystack so terribly hard to find?"

Rose had grown accustomed to the thorny silence of her suburban neighborhood. A much wished-for child, born of her parents' substantial posterity complex, she was doted upon by her elders & ceaselessly praised for her many talents. From an early age, she donned a frilly apron & served Chardonnay & light hors d'oeuvres to household visitors, later entertaining them with piano solos & poetic recitations. The question may here be raised whether in fact everything which is meant to happen *must*, but in this case, let us suspend our disbelief. Let us continue to imagine there are indeed inescapable fates. Rose's father did not want his only daughter confused by "unclean thoughts." Rose's mother did not want her only daughter tempted by "bodily desires." They feared Exposure as an unsafe place: kingdom overrun by beasts & briars. As a consequence, their child was not permitted to watch *Melrose Place* or venture far from the yard unattended. "You have the whole garden & a tetherball set. What more could any girl want?" But in the end, she found the window-well, breaking through its spidery glass. In the end, she found the high gate & pried the rusted padlock free, despite its camouflage of burrs & bees & lilacs. Like all children, she had a yearning to find the Terrible transformed to something magical—the Grotesque redeemed, the frog made beautiful on its own amphibian terms. She read *Siddhartha* & felt betrayed, but in the morning when she woke, for the first time she knew she was really awake: splintered as a sand dollar, unsure who to blame, but finally & truly awake.

Somewhere in the Heartland,

    or the Deep South,

some two (or three (or four discover the sticky mix of sex & vinyl))

                     curse the air conditioner   failed at a crucial moment

            And somewhere in the Pacific Northwest, in a ferryboat bathroom—

or New England, in an untended apple orchard, long past picking season—

                         these bodies:

bent the way of wind,
curled the way of bed

And the lie all lovers tell themselves, at least once, lapping easily in the inter-tide:

that we *invented* this, that what we do has never been done before, & never better

The hood. The wink. The smirk in the bedroom mirror.

What to make of the Rumpelstiltskin who emerges (in each of us) during these most intimate times?

What straw, what flax, have I transformed for you, Beloved—
What price will I exact in return?

This love—muddled by lust, enmeshed in compensation—with eyes shut tight or gaping wide, amazed
It seems   in the end   such a thing to ask:

No matter who you are to each other
No matter how many times you have asked before

I had seen *The Sound of Music* thirty-six times. Taped off network television onto static-thick VHS.

I was interested in becoming a nun like Fräulein Maria, or royalty like Baroness Schraeder.

I was interested in wearing a uniform & blowing a whistle & taking a wife.

I was interested in dancing during a rainstorm inside a glass-enclosed gazebo.

There was, however, a glitch in the tape where my father had tried to edit out commercials. Just before the culminating scene—Captain Von Trapp about to kiss (& shush) the still-crooning Fräulein Maria—a portion of a douche commercial cut in. A striking young woman wearing a flowered sundress & no shoes sat on her verandah playing the cello. The voiceover came through warbled, but the brand name was clear—*Summer's Eve*—which made sense given that it was also a summer's evening at the Austrian estate where Captain Von Trapp & Fräulein Maria professed their love, proclaiming they "must have done something good." In my mind, the two became conflated: douching & doing something good. Also: douching & playing the cello, another sound of music.

> **douche** *n.* a cleansing fluid flushed through the vagina as a hygienic measure; often used to purify a woman's body before or after intercourse.

"What does this mean?" passing the dictionary to my friend in fear.

"It's like a tampon," she replied. "If you use one, you're automatically *deflowered*."

"And that's wrong, right?"

Alicia, who wore bang-less black hair & purple leotards & attended an expensive School for the Gifted, stood tall on her toes, the tiny bones crackling, commanding my rapt attention:

"If you're not a virgin & you're not married, you might as well be a prostitute—or dead."

In sex education class, we are invited to write our anonymous questions on blue notecards & pass them forward for the teacher to answer:

What is the Maidenhead? I think it's a ship, but my sister says it's a bridge.

(I picture it, white sails shaking like the *Mayflower*: a dozen bright-white aprons hanging out to dry.)

"Actually, maidenhead is *not* a ship *or* a bridge. It's another word for *hymen*.

Does anyone know what *hymen* means?"

(I rack my brain, disliking the word, & the name *Regina*, & Brussel sprouts, which the word also reminds me of.)

"The hymen is a fold of tissue that partly covers the vagina of a virgin."

(Giggles all around, & Mrs. Kolbe chiding.)

My question, written in careful cursive: *Why does sex change people so completely?*

"Hmm," she murmurs, "I'm not sure how to respond to this one."
Shaking her head: "I'm sorry. I don't know what to say."

Are nuns Mrs.—since they're married to God—or Miss—since they don't get it on?

Will you really go to hell if you fornicate?

Can men be virgins too, or is there a different name?

(Giggles all around, & Mrs. Kolbe chiding.)

Alicia again, sitting cross-legged on her canopy bed, feet ceaselessly flexing:
"Did you know that vagina means *sheath*? And what does a sheath cover? A sword! Which
means the penis is a sword, & the body is a battlefield, & sex is a kind of war." Her brown
eyes round as buttons; her mouth breathless, gleaming.
"I thought that was *love*," I reply. "*Love* & war."
"I'm just saying," limbs shaking from too much sugar, too many ideas.
"But sheaths *protect* swords. A sword rests in a sheath when it isn't slaying dragons & other things of that
nature." (My new favorite phrase.) "You make it sound like men & women are doing battle with each other."
"They *are*, Dummy. That's why it's called *the battle of the sexes*."
"Why *what* is?"
"I'm just saying"—triumph in her tone—"I'm just saying."

For all we know, Rapunzel may have been a nun, & the castle tower just as easily a cloister. She may have
renounced all her worldly possessions, promised to live an obedient life, & solemnly sworn (on penalty of
death) never to sheath a lover's sword. This one, *celibacy's vow*: virginity raised to a higher power. She
may, however, have maintained one secret vanity, which over the years grew increasingly difficult to
conceal. Having once seen Crystal Gayle perform "Don't It Make My Brown Eyes Blue" at a country music
festival outside Paducah, KY, young Pun determined to grow her hay-colored hair equally long & lavish,

providing a curtain of warmth in the winter &, when tightly braided, a most efficient broom. One day as Rapunzel dutifully swept her Spartan cell, she was lured close to the window by a mischievous minstrel crooning a familiar song. Glimpsing her sturdy rope of hair, the minstrel called out, "Sister, why is your head not shaved like the others of your order?" Shamed by her sudden exposure, Rapunzel instructed the man to ascend via the rose trellis that adorned the cloister's walls, believing she might seduce him into silence. When he found this apparatus incomparably wobbly, she consented at last to lower her hair, which the man climbed eagerly, fitting his feet between each stair-like crevice of her braid. Upon reaching the ledge, however, the minstrel removed his cloak, revealing a priest's collar cinched tightly at his throat. Her breath choked in: quick gasps, hasty swallows. With one lithe stroke of a swiftly wielded knife, the priest severed Rapunzel's hair, which plummeted to the earth, unbinding in flight & scattering as sheaves of wheat among the birds assembled below. At the same moment, the bedside mirror cracked. Rapunzel reached for a shard of glass, wherein her brown eyes blazed suddenly, unabashedly, blue.

Somewhere in the soft Sandusky dusk:
                     Ferris wheel kisses, Kewpie dolls purchased with darts

                                          A tunnel of something resembling love
                              Or a funhouse mirror that mocks it

Past-Knowing Time:
                                the curfews of Kalamazoo & a triangle (something resembling love)
                        played out in voice box & speakers at the fast-food drive-thru

Even Anchorage, under siege of unrelenting solstice sun:

                                        what curtains cannot *curtail*
                                   what windows cannot *wind down*

Bear witness to the wilderness in each of us—
                      the howl of something human: that hunger sometimes resembling love

How to resist the myths of Honolulu,
Seduction's same old story set to a *Tropical Paradise* track: Waikiki, Hanauma Bay

here, not *certain*—

The sun sets in these nether-regions also, sinking below the horizon-line of *happily ever after*

                                              sand dollars split open
                                              spilling their white doves
                                              like those that clutter
                                              dingy Oahu streets

                    (*dove*, recall, is a kinder word for *pigeon*)

Stand in the Punchbowl. Gaze out over the massive sea. Remember Pearl Harbor. *Love & War.* Green geckos on white stucco walls. Limbs severed. Bodies splitting like hairs. The *technicalities* of Love. Of War. Recall how *once upon a time* you stood there, sixteen, hollow as a seashell, ocean of longing rushing through. Think of the astronauts, their white spacesuits, their copious quantities of Tang. *Above it all*— moon adorning the hood of their grand interstellar automobile, whirr of nothing but space all around. Imagine love being made without gravity. The unbinding, the scattering, the sheaves.

Heather & Sara were, plainly put, *different* from other girls.

          High school: all pleated plaid & aching recidivism.

"Did I see you, smoking after class? Did I see you, one torch passed between your angsty mouths?"

      What I really said (less nimble, less quick): "What makes you the way that you are?"

Sara shrugs. *I'm a pagan. Fuck these Puritans. Nuns don't like men either.*

"Can a lesbian still be a virgin?"
Sara chews her pen cap, tucks her hair.
   Depends. Has this hypothetical lesbian ever fucked a hypothetical girl?

"But how *could* she?"
   Depends. How do you define sex? How do you qualify fucking?

"I don't. I mean—I'm just curious."
   Don't be curious. (Light eyes shimmering, moist without tears.) *Be wise.*

   From my textbook[1]: *The vocation to chastity—the successful integration of sexuality within a person—is a common one to all people, no matter their state in life.*

   From my friend, the Feminist: *Abstinence is tricky.*

   From *Merriam-Webster*: *Abstention from unlawful sexual intercourse, or from all sexual intercourse; purity of conduct or intention; personal integrity.*

Me: "I'm saving myself."
   Her: "From what?"
Me: "Not from—*for.*"
   Her: "Why?"
Me: "Because . . . I have a lot of integrity (?)"
   Her: "Try again."
Me: "Because . . . it's morally right (?)"
   Her: "Gimme a break."
Me: "Because . . . I'm scared."
   Her: "Now we're getting somewhere."

There was once a titian-haired woman—fresh & foolhardy—mad with love for a certain man. They married young, conceived at once, & settled into a comfortable, uncomplicated life. Until the woman

---

[1] Kieran Sawyer, *Sex and the Teenager: Choices and Decisions* (Notre Dame: Ave Maria Press, 1990).

awoke at thirty, splintered as a sand dollar, unsure who to blame, *exile* flashing urgent as a flare. Lacking explanation or excuse, she packed her bags, bundled her child, & proceeded into the world alone: terrified to leave, more terrified not to. In the interim, she divorced, remarried, & divorced again, returning in the end to the same man she had loved since her seventeenth birthday.

"Are you finished now?" he asked.

"Not finished—*ready*," she said.

You have likely heard of *crossing the bridge, bridging the gap, burning the bridge,* & water flowing beneath it: bygones, be gone! You may wonder in retrospect if all these examples refer to the same bridge & whether you would jump from it if the one you love most in the world asked you to. You may consider yourself by this time quite an expert in bridges, whether drawbridges flexed for passing ships, or rope bridges frayed at their seams & shaking. You may think *Golden Gate* or *Brooklyn* or crest of your nose or rise of your mouth or a card game you've never played before.

This   That   The Other   All of the Above

(circle one)

You may also remember the troll living under the bridge, that *same* bridge, site of your most flagrant hesitations. Maybe this troll is a gruff city maintenance worker who carries his lunch in a sturdy black box & drinks coffee from a rusted canteen. Or maybe he's a nomad camped in a furrowed tent, or a vagrant hopeful for change. Maybe *he* is a *she*. Maybe the troll is a figment of your imagination, fickle & prone to complain. Traditionally, this story is told from the perspective of three billy goats who trick the troll into letting them pass. A psychologist may ask: "What was their motivation for crossing the bridge? Was their behavior reinforced or thwarted?" A businessman may ask: "What were the bargaining strategies they used? How did the goats profit from their passage?" A poet, however, may be prompted to consider the troll more closely—*why was he there? what threat did he pose?* Maybe *he* is a *she.* The possibilities become metaphorical at this stage. What if you are all three of the billy goats—the psychologist would be pressed to classify them, *Id, Ego, Superego,* but we will refrain—& what if you are also the troll? Is it startling to consider yourself the protagonist *&* the antagonist of your own story? The businessman might call this a *monopoly* (on pleasure, on worry, on pain). But you are also the bridge-builder—the one crossing above, the one guarding below—& the shadows their bodies cast, & the grassy knoll the goats are headed toward, & the water (an ocean of longing perhaps?) that rushes, endlessly, under the bridge you have made. A fortune cookie may thus conclude: *Look before you leap, but close your eyes, falling.*

Somewhere in a
      Courtyard Marriott
           jacuzzi suite
(replete with complimentary fruit basket & untouched Champagne),

        the legend of the First Time begins to break down

Elsewhere:
        a Weston or a Hilton or a Radisson

This is the story I was groomed for:

      One man, one woman, a diamond plus two gold bands, three to four years of waiting
    Meals of mashed potatoes, in-laws-to-be, the gravy of close scrutiny & small conversation
                Purity of conduct & intention

Rebuttals (unspoken, unheard):

White is not my best color.
I hate waiting.

I did not want to be an "anything *but*" girl. I wanted to be an "everything *&*."

      But this is the way that God intended, & we'll be blessed for following His commands . . .
                I want it to be special, to be sacred . . .
           It's safer this way—no risk, no room for regret . . .

Sometimes still I yearn to believe the story of the Holy Sacrament of Marriage. I want to drive to Boston now, in a fervor, or head north with passports in hand to Toronto: *the warm evening saying Step, anywhere you go is yours.*[2] Would it be redundant now, after all the years of—what would you call this love—*improvisation*? I read what the Poet says, & I believe her: *to bloom is to be taken completely.*

---

[2] Several fragments in this section are borrowed gratefully from *Hybrids of Plants and of Ghosts* by Jorie Graham
(Princeton University Press, 1980).

There is no man here, no heart-shaped tub in the Poconos, no cufflinks in the bureau drawer. The woman in this story, who could have been me—who I could have been—finds rose petals on her pillow most pleasing, & the large bouquet in the foyer, the handfuls of crisp money & the tables of shiny packages, the *praise*—all of it, most pleasing. She loves him of course. This *is* what they have been waiting for, & now the whole world of their knowing blesses them, & the hotel manager shakes his hand & smiles on her with a face warmed by full approval. Why then does she tremble at the unexpected weight of the second ring? Alone now, temptation diffused by endorsement, by two signatures with a wobbly pen & the State of Wherever pronouncing them . . .

She never imagined this part of the story: *dénouement*: disappointment, fatigue. Her shining moment on the red carpet with the white satin dress & the dark muslin sash has passed. Fräulein Maria returns from the honeymoon altered. Where is her feisty spirit now, her knack for mischief & spontaneity? She no longer rides bicycles, juggles apples in the market square, tips over boats in the bay. Is it contentment, complacency? Why the veiled look in her eyes, the glowing acquiescence?

He stands at the sink, having done what he was supposed to do, having become a man of patience, of *personal integrity*. And this is his reward. He doesn't want to think of her as a prize, but how not to covet what is consistently denied? *White petals, creaseless, ambitious.* He feels the undertow of all her expectations, the hard grip of the hotel manager's hand, the new weight of his unchanged name. The words rain down on him now: etiquette, entitlement: *may I break your even weave, loosen your knot?* Questions of ownership, enlightenment: what does she want from me? what may I take from her?

The axis of rupture around which this hour revolves: *if I break you, are you mine?*

It will be like "The Little Mermaid," but not the Disney version. In the real story, which I read as a child, she falls in love with a prince, trading her voice for a pair of legs. But the legs do not simply appear. They must grow painfully, replacing her fishtail, leaving her vulnerable there in the inter-tide where she may just as likely drown.

Spooning, the first time:
our bodies, long & sharp as knives

Swimming, which she has known all her life by another name, becomes suddenly difficult, foreign.

Unbuttoning my sweater in the stuffy dorm:
Why won't you touch them? You're a man. You're supposed to want to touch them.

Nothing works out according to plan. Her desire is not returned; her passions are not reciprocated.

"What do you want?"
Thinking a long time: "Does it matter?"

The failed seduction carries a penalty. She cannot remain human, & she cannot return to the sea. Not as she was. Water now, flooding the bridge.

Playing chess again, with the one I most wanted to love:
"Is this it, then? No more movement. Every piece has already been played."
He said it, with a grand gesture & a sigh—
Stalemate—& gingerly kissed my eyes.

The no-longer mermaid, no-longer maiden will dissolve from her hybrid state. She will be transformed into the deadly cold sea-foam of the Arctic Sea.

What will become of me? I wondered.
Not a virgin like my aunt,   or a mother like my mother

spinster *n.* archaic term for a professional thread spinner & by extension for a woman who never marries or raises children because she can support herself with her work, thereby having no need to marry.

Miss   Mrs.   Ms.   Mr.

(circle one)

Think of the hay, the straw, the flax, the gold. Think of dallying, tumbling—the needle of light spearing the hay-loft window. Think of cornfields & cornflowers: all those husked bodies, those seeded fields. Think of Big Bone Lick State Park (because the landscape has humor) & Barren River (because it has sorrow also). Think of the ancient green hills, many-siloed. Think of the mad couplings, & the cover of darkness, & the prayers that congregate (unspoken, unheard) in the deep basin of the wishing well. Think of lust, abstention, power. Think of our finest approximations, that something resembling love.

The Renunciation

What if the Woman did not consent, regardless of betrothal or virginity, regardless of the Angel's divine demand? What if Mary Ann, alone in the family farmhouse on the outskirts of Iowa City, sat drinking an RC Cola & stitching her mother's shift? There were socks to darn also, & blankets to mend, & in the background, a crackling television set: canned game show laughter & toothpaste commercial jingles. "I have a steady boyfriend," she said. "I have two years left of high school, & after that, who knows?" "I'm thinking about Rhode Island School of Design." "I've never even seen the Ocean." And finally, growing weary of the charade: "Listen, I don't want kids." The Angel persisted, but the Girl was firm. She stood up, her thin frame drowning in the button-down dress, her bare feet with toenails gleaming. "I'm really flattered, but I'd rather not. Here," gesturing to the tattered screen door, the sprawling front porch—"let me show you out." Gabriel might as well have been a traveling salesman, sleek car brimming with encyclopedias or household cleaners. He might as well have worn a suit with dark tie slightly askew & shoes polished so bright she could see her face in them when she looked down. Mary Ann knew where the shotgun was, but she didn't think she'd need it. She slipped on an apron, pockets full of pegs, & walked around back to the clothesline. There was laundry to take in, & more to be washed, & later that night she had plans to watch *WKRP in Cincinnati* . . .

The Rorschach

"If I say body—"
"Husk."
"If I say spirit—"
"Light."
"If I say light—"
"Mirror."
"Mirror—"
"Fog."
"What about crux?"
"Possible."
"What about climax?"
"Over."
"Purity—"
"Futile."

            "Futility—"
"Pure."
            "Now you're playing with me."
"Maybe."
            "Body—"
"Soft."
            "Hay—"
"Sex."
            "Sex—"
"Multi-valent."
            "Come again?"
"*Exactly*."
            "Why?"
"X."
            "As in former?"
"As in female."
            "Bridge—"
"Passage."
            "Safe—"
"Reluctant."
            "Save—"
"Hoard."
            "Hoard—"
"Lonely."
            "Light—"
"Winnow."
            "Kiss—"
"Linger."
            "Fallow—"
"Earth."
            "God—"
"Fog."
            "Chaste—"
"Antiquate."
            "Religion—"
"Apostasy."

"Iron—"

"Maiden."

"Maiden—"

"Red."

"Music—"

"Ocean."

"Body—"

"Story."

"Virgin—"

"Seashell."

"Story—"

"Golden."

"Truth—"

"Tenuous."

"Safe—"

"Red."

MEZZANINE

Let us join our program in-progress.

Or—as our protagonist might say—*in medias res.*

Overall, the entresol is not the best view in the house. Some say it's preferable to the ground. Others, I'm told, would trade their nosebleeds in a heartbeat for the chance to sit further down.

In the thick of things, she says. *In the deep, semantic swampland.*

"Dammit, Poet, mind your manners!"

The trouble begins here: *fallacy of the undistributed middle.*

> FIRST PREMISE: All poets are unscientific
> SECOND PREMISE: This protagonist is unscientific
> (Syllogistic Fallacy): *Therefore*, this protagonist is a poet

The protagonist cannot be proved a poet. In this particular logical fallacy, the middle term ("unscientific") is undistributed because neither of its uses ("all poets," "this protagonist") applies to all unscientific persons.

A valid syllogism is as follows:

> FIRST PREMISE: All poets are unscientific
> SECOND PREMISE: This protagonist is a poet
> (Categorical Syllogism): *Therefore*, this protagonist is unscientific

"Let me see your résumé, Poet."

                        "I don't have a *resume* as such."

"Well, what have you?"

                        "Curriculum vita."

"Always with the Latin."

                        "Excuse me?"

"One question: can you *do* much?"

                        "Long as it's not scientific."

Hi, my name is Joe, I've got a wife, three kids, & I work in a button factory. One day, my boss came

THE INTERVIEW

"You seem to have a lot of letters after your name."

                        (Nod, cross legs)

"Would it be fair to say you are *overly* educated?"

                        (Flush, uncross legs)

"You are aware this is a *staff* position, not *faculty*?"

                        (Nod, flush, cross legs)

"You will be responsible for making coffee, sorting mail . . ."

                        (Nod, flush, uncross legs)

"These are esteemed scientists & mathematicians."

(Nod, rise, shake hands, smile)

Walk into the bathroom & scream.

THE ORIENTATION

"One of your primary duties will be taking dictation for a professor who does not operate computers."

"Yes. An *amanuensis*. I look forward to it."

"Amana-what?"

"It means a stenographer, a person skilled in the transcription of speech."

"So, a *secretary?*"

"Sort of—It's a more precise, more interesting word."

"*Ms. Wade*, you'll find that we in this department are not *interested* in interesting words."

THE DEBRIEFING

Of course, it didn't actually happen this way. This is the portion known as *poetic license*. Everyone was kind. Nothing out of the ordinary. A few times the question was raised: "So, with all your schooling, shouldn't you be teaching somewhere?"

The Kenning Repertory production of Mezzanine *was first performed in Pittsburgh, Pennsylvania, in July 2004. The play was directed by the story's protagonist & cast according to equal opportunity employment guidelines. The play is ongoing, the poet persistently unscientific.*

Time: THE PRESENT
Setting: THE OFFICE

[*Interior, Day.*]

"I'm a little confused here where you say *math is the universal language.*"

"What's confusing about it?"

"Well, I thought *emotion* was."

"*Affect.*"

"So you agree?"

"No. I'm just pointing out that in our lexicon, emotion is conveyed as affect."

"Same difference, isn't it?"

"I don't follow."

"I don't lead."

"About the *same* difference? How is that possible?"

"It's an expression, Sir—an *idiom.*"

"In our lexicon, we recognize 'no difference' & 'just noticeable difference.'"

jnd *n. smallest difference in a specified modality of sensory input that is detectable by a human being or other animal; also known as the "difference limen" or "differential threshold."*

"But that's binary thinking, isn't it?"

"Correct."

"Do you prefer *discrete* over *continuous*?"

"Do you prefer *intuitive* over *significant*?"

"Do you have health benefits?"

"Naturally."

"Are you salaried as opposed to hourly?"

"Naturally."

"Do you own instead of rent?"

"Yes."

"Invest instead of scrimp/save/spend?"

"I don't follow."

"I don't lead."

Time: THE PRESENT
Setting: THE HOME

[*Interior, Night.*]

"I know what you're up to."

"Do you?"

"You're stealing fire from the gods."

"Which is code for—?"

"Stealing language from the scientists."

(Shrug, smile): "My poem has to get made somehow."

& said, "Hey Joe, are you busy?" I said, "No." He said, "Turn this button with your right hand."

FIRST PREMISE: All universities are ivory towers
SECOND PREMISE: Babel is a tower
(Syllogistic Fallacy): *Therefore*, Babel is a university

FIRST PREMISE: All universities are ivory towers
SECOND PREMISE: Babel is a university
(Categorical Syllogism): *Therefore*, Babel is an ivory tower

Time: THE PRESENT
Setting: THE OFFICE

[*Interior, Day.*]

"I think we're suffering from a confusion of tongues: an interdisciplinary deficit."

"Of course you do. Words are your currency."

"Words are *everyone's* currency, Sir."

"Wrong! Numbers are. Lest you forget: *math is money.*"

"Dirty money."

"How do you figure?"

"Numbers lie."

"Poets lie."

"I have a license. Where's yours?"

"What are we even babbling about?"

"Brooks babble, Sir. Poets inquire."

"Poets *circumlocute*."

Time: THE PRESENT
Setting: THE HOME

[*Interior, Night.*]

"Do you think I tend to circumlocute?"

"Hmmm . . . let me see . . . do you employ roundabout speaking for poetic effect?"

"There's a word for that!" (triumphant)
"*Periphrasis.*"

"Is there a word for people who are *plagued* with it?"

"No, but there is a wage."

"Is it *minimum*?"

"It isn't *maximum*."

"Don't forget about your student loans. Grace period's more like a comma."

Hi, my name is Joe, I've got a wife, three kids, & I work in a button factory. One day, my boss came

Time: THE PRESENT
Setting: THE CEREBRUM

[*Deep Interior, Deep Night.*]

Perhaps I should have been a plumber. They make good money. More than I'll ever make, that's for sure. I wish they paid you per hour what you could type per minute. I'd make $96.00 every 60 minutes, which is almost as much as a counseling psychologist, though not nearly as much as a criminal lawyer. Where did that dream go? I loved Ben Matlock & the white suits & the ceaseless storytelling. I was all primed for Perry Mason, so how did I end up a dead-end Della Street—minus the frilly collars & unreasonably pointed shoes? I like animals. I could have been a vet or a marine biologist. I like teeth. I could have been a dentist. How am I here, in this ambiguous field: "Humanities"? Surely it isn't because I like "humans" so much. (Or is it?) Why not an anthropologist then, if that's the plea I meant to bargain? But the truth is: I'm after the "dorsal" & "ventral," "pileated," "crenellated," "sessile," & "motile." I'm after "bicuspids," "incisors," the "pulp," the "gum," the "cementum." Language, you see, is what I've been stalking. Words—colorful as Easter eggs, piling up & piling up, jostling each against the other inside this sturdy basket.

FIRST PREMISE: All important people have vocations
SECOND PREMISE: Poets have vocations
(Syllogistic Fallacy): *Therefore*, poets are important people

What would it take to make it true?

FIRST PREMISE: All important people have vocations
SECOND PREMISE: Poets are important people
(Categorical Syllogism): *Therefore*, poets have vocations

& said, "Hey Joe, are you busy?" I said, "No." He said, "Turn this button with your left hand."

Time: THE PRESENT
Setting: THE OFFICE
[*Interior, Day.*]

76

"I notice in these transcripts you actually type out *square root* every time I say *square root*."

"Yes?"

"Well, it's a symbol."

"It's also a word. Two words, in fact."

"Do you not know what a square root symbol looks like?"

"No. I know. It's the little funny check mark that extends over another number—a kind of numeric carport."

"In the future, when you hear the phrase *square root*, please use the symbol, not the phrase."

"What have you got against the letters?"

"It's not proper mathematical notation. The symbol is more concise & more accurate."

"Can you calculate the square root of *anything*?"

"Certainly."

"Anything at all?"

"Absolutely."

"OK then. What about the square root of wonderful?"

"I beg your pardon?"

"Are you saying you can't calculate the square root of wonderful, Sir?"

"This is nonsense. No one can."

"Carson McCullers did. Back in 1958. Calculated it brilliantly."

"And who the Dickens is he?"

"Now Dickens—he was good, too. But you must remember, Sir: Dickens was from a different time."

Time: THE PRESENT
Setting: THE HOME

[*Interior, Night.*]

"Get the calculator."

"My three least favorite words in the language."

"No joke, Julie. Gas went up again. It's $416.00 to pay it off in full, or $196.00 if we take the budget plan."

"What does that mean?"

"It means we pay $196.00 every month all year, even in the summer when we're not using any heat at all."

"We're not *really* poor, you know. It's just a tight spot; it's only temporary."

"I know, Pollyanna"—warm arm around my shoulder—"I know."

[*Exterior, Night.*]

Snow, snow, snow. Expensive, elegant snow.

Hi, my name is Joe, I've got a wife, three kids, & I work in a button factory. One day, my boss came

FIRST PREMISE: All failures constitute debt
SECOND PREMISE: The poet finds herself indebted
(Syllogistic Fallacy): *Therefore,* the poet is a failure

FIRST PREMISE: All failures constitute debt
SECOND PREMISE: The poet is a failure
(Categorical Syllogism): *Therefore,* the poet finds herself indebted

Time: THE PRESENT
Setting: THE OFFICE

[*Interior, Day.*]

"Are you familiar with *tautology*?"

"Yes. Are you familiar with *anaphora*?"

Time: THE PRESENT
Setting: THE CEREBRUM

[*Deep Interior, Deep Night.*]

I wonder if it's possible to specialize yourself into obscurity, to render yourself obsolete. And which is considered more valuable—breadth or depth of knowledge? And who makes more—the competent generalist or the certified expert? And how do you know when your apprenticeship is over? How do you know when your mastery has actually begun?

[*Turn down heat; add extra blankets to the bed.*]

Is it arrogant to want to teach? (Masochistic? Ill-considered?) Is teaching in fact the alternative to "doing," like the old adage suggests? I'm not in danger of any profound specialization—yet what canon can I claim as my own? It's such a lie, this Master's level: "post-baccalaureate," "pre-doctoral." Who was it invented these words?

[*Sit on the stairs; rub the static-filled backs of the cats; slip on a jacket.*]

What do I know? This is serious now.

What   do   I   actually   know?

Am I just a dilettante—all lofty words & no real substance?
Am I just suspended here, somewhere between the floor & ceiling?

jnd *n. smallest difference in a specified modality of sensory input that is detectable by a human being or other animal; also known as the "difference limen" or "differential threshold."*

& said, "Hey Joe, are you busy?" I said, "No." He said, "Turn this button with your right foot."

Time: THE PRESENT
Setting: THE OFFICE

[*Interior, Day.*]

> "Do you think all anaphora is necessarily
> tautological?"

"Do you have my copies?"

> "Yes. 25 packets. Stapled. Double-sided."

"And anaphora is—that chorus effect in poems?"

> "That's one way of looking at it. Yes. I like that.
> Anaphora functions as a kind of refrain, usually
> at the beginning of successive lines or stanzas."

"And would you email this itinerary to the other panelists?"

> "Certainly."

"I see no reason to assume that redundancy is a fixed corollary of repetition. Do you?"

"No reason at all."

"On the other hand"—switching his withered finger—"everyone hates a gimmick, even the most highly effective ones."

"Those in particular, Sir."

FIRST PREMISE: All knowledge is inherently incomplete
SECOND PREMISE: Poets are especially attuned to incompleteness
(Syllogistic Fallacy): *Therefore*, poets possess knowledge

FIRST PREMISE: All knowledge is inherently incomplete
SECOND PREMISE: Poets possess knowledge
(Categorical Syllogism): *Therefore*, poets are inherently incomplete

Hi, my name is Joe, I've got a wife, three kids, & I work in a button factory. One day, my boss came

Time: THE PRESENT
Setting: THE HOME

[*Interior, Day.*]

"Now I know why people love weekends so much."

"Is there anything better? Stay in bed
until ten, eat flapjacks, watch VH1. Pretend you
have nothing better to do."

"I'm tired from the week, you know. It wears me down. I feel like I spend half of Saturday just recovering."

"We do."

"So—you think you'll get a PhD?"

"I'm not sure I can afford to be that useless."

"Stop. You don't mean it."

"I was a senior in high school. Nuns
telling me every day how *full of promise* I was. But
what did that mean? Promise to do *what*? I've spent
the last decade in college learning that I'm *able* to
learn, that I *like* learning, that I have an *aptitude*
for it. But have I made good on that promise? Have
I accomplished *anything*? Do I have any verifiable
skills?

"Well, you do make—*the best*—apple cinnamon flapjacks I have ever tasted."

(My jaw relaxing—a smile at last.) "Perhaps I have
missed my calling then. Too much time in the
classroom, not enough time in the kitchen."

& said, "Hey Joe, are you busy?" I said, "No." He said, "Turn this button with your left foot."

THE BACK-STORY

Pre-Script
There are two peculiar attributes of back-stories. One is the *shared universe* phenomenon, wherein several sto-
rytellers exchange characters & settings, often referencing events that have taken place in others' stories. The
second is called *retroactive continuity*, wherein new information is added to "historical" material, deliberately
changing previously established facts in a work of serial fiction. *Facts—in fiction.* Enjoy them.

In 1997, I wrote my first poems of the modern era. My professor was a poet, self-professed. He liked
Auden & Whitman. I liked them, too. We read "As I Walked Out One Evening," & it sang to me the way
enchanted salmon trilled through the flooded streets. The poem was a song inside a song. I knew it at once.
Unscientific—but certain. Intuitive—*&* significant.

Side-Note
This poem also is a song inside a song.

I believed all things were possible in poetry. Difficult truths could be voiced & mourned. Rivers could leap over mountains. Glaciers could cut through walls. I felt I loved poetry, with the best of my crooked heart; that I wanted to write it, till the ocean was folded & hung up to dry.

Side-Note
My heart is still crooked. The ocean still wide, wet, & full.

When my first portfolio came back to me—those pages of words honeyed with optimism, sticky to their corners with warm, excessive sweetness—the teacher had written only one line. A question. It was, in retrospect, rather "poetic" of him.

Do you also believe for every drop of rain that falls a flower grows?

What I should have said:

It would be impossible to calculate or denote precisely how much rain is required for a single flower to grow, & at what rate, & for what duration.

What I did say:

Nothing. Not a single word.

End-of-term advice:

You have strong verbal skills. You clearly enjoy language. You might be able to make it as a fiction writer, but don't kid yourself about the poems.

What I should have said:

How do you know that poetry isn't fiction? There are embedded stories, one inside the other; there are falsehoods.

What I did say:

Nothing. Not a single word.

jnd *n. smallest difference in a specified modality of sensory input that is detectable by a human being or* *other animal; also known as the "difference limen" or "differential threshold."*

Hi, my name is Joe, I've got a wife, three kids, & I work in a button factory. One day, my boss came

THE FRONTISPIECE

Pre-Script
It is important to note that the definition of this term is, like most terms, highly context-dependent. In architecture, for instance, it suggests *an ornamental façade* or *a small pediment atop a door or window*. In literature, however, it suggests *an illustration that faces or immediately precedes the title page of a book*.

> FIRST PREMISE: All architecture involves façade
> SECOND PREMISE: All literature also involves façade
> (Syllogistic Fallacy): *Therefore*, literature & architecture are related fields
>
> FIRST PREMISE: All architecture involves façade
> SECOND PREMISE: Literature & architecture are related fields
> (Categorical Syllogism): *Therefore*, all literature also involves façade

Things you should know about me, things I should have told you at the outset:

I talk too much & too fast & am prone to thinking out loud.

I require a certain amount of credible delusion to maintain my robust & congenial nature.

*I have never understood the plot of a single *James Bond* movie.*

I test hopelessly "average" on standardized tests.

I was once admitted to a doctoral program in "Mythological Studies." Santa Barbara was beautiful, but I couldn't afford to go.

I always believed I would be a first-rate gumshoe, & at one time, an exceptional scientist.

I never made it past trigonometry, but I surprised a math teacher once with my prowess at inductive proofs.

I once sold shoes on commission for a JC Penney store, & in peak season, made more than I do now.

*I have been told, & on more than one occasion, that I make *the best* apple cinnamon flapjacks.*

I consider "alleged" the most significant word in our language.

& said, "Hey Joe, are you busy?" I said, "No." He said, "Turn this button with your tongue."

Time: THE PRESENT
Setting: THE HOME

[*Interior, Night.*]

"We're going to have to cut back."

"If we give up cable, we lose the $5.00 a month Showtime deal."

"I know. That's how they keep us loyal."

"I'd really hate to lose *Weeds.*"

"Remember when we could afford to *buy* weed?"

"It cost more than $5.00, though."

"Point taken . . . What about the landline? Is that really necessary?"

"For dial-up, it is."

"Maybe we could find a cheap package & switch to DSL."

"Maybe. But there might be an installation fee."

"Undoubtedly."

"And health insurance?"

"Even without cable, it's still too high."

"I miss the Student Health Center already."

"So just know this: we can't get hurt, unless it's in the car."

"We're not *really* poor, you know."

"I know."

"We work hard, we pay our bills, we enjoy all kinds of little luxuries. Free coffee at work, sometimes whole catered lunches . . ."

"Julie, *I know*. I'm not blaming you. Does it feel like I'm blaming you?"

"No. I just—wish we didn't have to worry is all."

"Did you know most Americans consider themselves *middle-class*?"

"I've heard that."

"I think this is what it means: being stuck in the middle. You have too much not to have to maintain it, & too little to ever get ahead."

Time: THE PRESENT
Setting: THE OFFICE

[*Interior, End of the Business Day.*]

"Are you on your way out?"

"Well, I try to catch the 5:13 bus."

"Oh, maybe tomorrow then . . ."

"Was there something you needed?"

"No. I just wanted—"

"You just wanted—" (glancing at the clock)

"To show you this."

"What is it?"

"It's a poem." (clarifying) "I didn't write it."

"But you found it?"

"It's something to read anyway, on the bus ride home."

Time: THE PRESENT
Setting: THE BUS

[*Interior, End of the Business Day.*]

"What's that?"

"From *Quarterly*. My boss gave it to me."

"The mad scientist? Let me see."

"'Transcription,' by Barbara Crooker."

"I've never heard of her."

"Neither have I."

On this blue day, I want to be
nothing more than an amanuensis
to the birds, transcribing all the bits
& snatches of song riding in on the wind.

And for that moment, there was nothing else to say.

jnd n. smallest difference in a specified modality of sensory input that is detectable by a human being or other animal; also known as the "difference limen" or "differential threshold."

Hi, my name is Joe, I've got a wife, three kids, & I work in a button factory. One day, my boss came

THE PENUMBRA PARABLE

There are a few complementary definitions to consider, such as *partial shadow between regions of complete darkness & complete illumination*; such as *outlining or surrounding region, peripheral to the main*; such as *area in which something exists to a lesser or uncertain degree, where distinction; or resolution is difficult or unlikely*; such as *extension of protection, reach, application, or consideration.* Multi-valent meanings. Enjoy them.

There once was a courtyard at the center of which sprawled a serpentine maze bordered by hedges. Around the fringes of the courtyard bloomed a variety of meta-fictional flowers, including (but not limited to) *Futility, Dogma, Hercules, Sisyphus, Auxiliary, Entropy, Camaraderie, Upward-Mobility, Prometheus, Obscurant, Innovation, Icarus, Relapse, Stagnation,* & *Big Cheese.* From a large crowd of academics assembled in the courtyard, two participants were strategically selected: one, a Scientist, the other, a Poet.

The Master of Ceremonies, who held joint Master's degrees in Business Administration & Sociology, commenced with the following instructions:

"Your goal, fine thinkers, is to work collaboratively to decipher this document"—waving a yellowed scroll—"which in turn will guide you through yonder labyrinth toward your combined reward."

Receiving the document, the Scientist remarked: "It seems we have been handed a useful heuristic."

Examining the document, the Poet concluded: "It seems we have been handed a treasure map."

"Heuristic."

"Treasure map."

"*Heuristic.*"

"*Treasure map.*"

As their argument enflamed, the Master of Ceremonies suggested that perhaps the dispute was one of nomenclature as opposed to ideology. "Is it not possible," the MC proposed, "that the document I have given you is both a heuristic & a treasure map?"

"A heuristic," the Scientist described, "is most simply understood as a method employing experimentation, evaluation, & trial-&-error to learn, discover, understand, or solve problems."

"A treasure map," the Poet declared, "is also a method employing experimentation, evaluation, & trial-&-error in pursuit of conquest or reward."

Agreeing it was in their best interest to collaborate rather than compete, the Scientist & the Poet proceeded into the shade of the maze & beyond the view of the growing crowd.

"Tell me something," the Scientist said, as they had been walking in silence for quite some time. "I've always wondered whether poets hypothesize."

"Certainly!" the Poet pronounced. "Poems are generated much the way I imagine experiments are. They begin with a guess or a question. Assumptions are tested. Expectations assessed. In a sense then, each poem *is* a hypothesis."

They continued walking & thinking & after a spell, the Poet inquired, "I too am curious. Are scientists inclined to improvise?"

"Certainly!" the Scientist exclaimed. "Devising experiments is every bit as creative & adventurous a process as developing poems. Consider the null hypothesis that cannot be rejected. Do we stop there, or do we push forward? Do we accept that all is random, or do we explore alternatives that might yield significance?"

"Would it be fair to say then," the Poet surmised, "that there is an element of surprise inherent in each of our endeavors?"

"Yes," the Scientist agreed, "I believe that is fair to say." Pausing: "Also, it seems both enterprises involve an element of risk & a possibility of failure."

"Yes," the Poet replied. "We are both engaged in risky & surprising business."

Before long, the intrepid pair, employing a combination of experimentation, evaluation, & trial-&-error, deduced a direct yet scenic pathway through the labyrinth & into a related field. There, a shovel awaited them, & an X of sheared grass indicated the place they should dig for their prize.

They took turns digging, for the box was buried deep, & when at last they lifted it out of the ground & raised the ancient lid upon its creaking hinges, what they found inside both amazed & bewildered them. Not extravagant enough to be *Faberge*, not familiar enough to be *Easter*, not blue enough to be *robin's* or mottled enough to be *quail's*: this ovate structure—profuse in color, matte-finished, smooth-textured— came stemmed with a curious message: *Behold, the curate's egg, the culmination of every maze.*

"Shall we crack it?" the Scientist suggested.

"I'm not sure," the Poet replied. "Perhaps we should retain it entire for symbolic purposes."

"Much like a piggy bank," the Scientist proposed, "its true worth may be concealed within."

As they debated the virtues of the seen & unseen, the whole & its parts, functional versus aesthetic forms of value, a great gust of wind whistled down through the trees & swept the egg from their hands. Thudding to the earth, it split open, & before them lay three quite ordinary objects, each one half-lustrous, half-dull.

"*Rock*," the Poet said, fingering the dark, hard aggregate of minerals.

"*Scissors*," the Scientist observed, raising the two pivoted blades by their metallic handle.

"*Paper*," they remarked in unison, lifting the single sheet of lined loose-leaf with its faint red margin & three holes evenly spaced down the left side. In sparse stick letters, an anonymous author had printed:

NOW YOU KNOW EVERYTHING

There was no time for awe or confusion then. Commence the *partial solar eclipse*, wherein the penumbra of the moon's shadow passes over a region of the earth's surface. The crowd had assembled again to celebrate this intermittent phenomenon, & the paper with its riddle, the rock with its durable weight, & the scissors with their great utility, in the course of these festivities were lost.

Only one thing remained to be done. Having cracked the curate's egg, having mastered the maze only to enter a new world of more pressing mysteries—namely:

WHAT IS IT WE KNOW?

(&)

HOW HAVE WE LEARNED IT?

(&)

WHY IS OUR KNOWING NEVER ENOUGH?

The Master of Ceremonies requested that all members of all departments of the University, & all practitioners of every trade & form of labor, stand together, raise their glasses, & drink a toast to their collective work. And the toast, which was familiar to most, reflected best the measurable significance of every arduous enterprise & went almost exactly like this:

You put your whole self in, you put your whole self out

You put your whole self in, & you shake it all about

You do the hokey pokey, & you turn yourself around

That's what it's all about

Time: THE PRESENT
Setting: THE CEREBRUM

[Deep Interior, Deep Night.]

The snow makes everything brighter. I'm awake thinking about taxes: dreaming a big refund this year, dreading the paperwork that must precede it. I heat up the little red kettle in this poetic (or is it scientific?) "darkest hour"—fulcrum between dusk & dawn. Snow so deep; the white anaphora (or is it tautology?) pure homage to Poet Frost. When I turn restless these slow winter nights, I reach for what I know best: rhythm of the seasons, rise & fall, proverb of the long-sequestered seed. Here in the entresol, the interstice; here in the thick of things, the deep, semantic swampland. Credit & debt. Curfew & bet. Curate's conundrum of risk & surprise. I tell myself, "Calm down." I tell myself, "You can only do so much." I remind myself of promises yet to keep, & miles still before sleep.

& said, "Are you busy?" I said, "Yes."

NULL

Hey, Nancy Drew, how are you?
Just fine, Caroline, have you any clues?

Artifacts:

- one big box in the Arlington basement marked *In Case of Apocalypse*
- twelve assorted-color condoms from the dance studio dressing room
- three Playtex Slimfits mixed in with the Jenga pieces
- six Polaroids (stacked like playing cards) atop the bedside table

What's your story, Morning Glory?
What's your tale, Nightingale?

Instructions:

- come to the front door, knock three times
- if someone answers, ask for a cup of sugar—always be polite so as not to arouse suspicion!
- if no answer, slip around back; climb in through the kitchen window
- sit down at the baby grand
- press the far left pedal called the "soft pedal" (not to be confused with the "damper")
- the keys will slide over to your right, leaving a visible gap
- look for the note, folded in fourths, tucked between the shiny ivories
- if no note there, try unlocking the grandfather clock (key should be in the door)
- place your hand under the face & reach up inside for the scroll

Cinderella, dressed in yella, went downstairs to kiss her fella,
Made a mistake & kissed a snake, how many doctors did it take?

There's a word for this, too. *Katabasis.*

           I was always an "avid reader," a "Book It!" superstar. (So many Personal Pan Pizzas—)

     Define as: *descent, journey downward*

                         Define as: *technical term for a visit to the underworld*

        Point of interest: *a hero is not a hero until/unless he has braved a katabasis*

Back in the days of our youth, when Joy & Kristin & I were all burgeoning sleuths
     (*poets who didn't even know it*)   for the Wade Detective Agency—later renamed the Silver
Swans after a Chinese restaurant in Burien & because all three of us liked birds . . .

Back in those days, when Joy was still Jewish, which meant she didn't love Jesus the same as we did &
my parents were still Lutheran like Martin Luther who loved his *Tannenbaum*
     (*Evergreen ablaze with candles*) . . .

And Kristin saw angels watching over her bed, with big wings & ballet slippers
     (The Arlingtons were Baptist: lots of seraphim & cherubim—but very little dancing)

At the Casey Treat revival center, I sit up straight in my nautical dress & try my best to pay attention

     Catch Phrases:

- the End Times
- the Great Tribulation

Bumper sticker on a minivan, armed to the teeth with children:

- *During Rapture, this vehicle will be unmanned*

There's a word for this, too. *Eschatology*

I had to spell it once for a particularly grueling Spelling Bee.

E·S·C

Define as: *study of last things*

Define as: *understanding or doctrine of the eschaton, or ultimate destiny of the world*

H·A·T

Stalling: "Could you use it in a sentence please?"

"The Second Coming is an important part of Christian *eschatology*, the theology concerned with the final events of human history & the fulfillment of the Messianic Prophesy."

O·L·O·G·Y

It's like this. Because Kristin always knew what things were like. *Remember how in the beginning of the Bible God is the Word? Well, the End Times are God getting to have His say. They're His Last Word.*

I asked Joy if she was concerned about the Afterlife. She said *no*. I asked if she worried about the fate of her soul. She said *not usually*. I asked if she had problems with faith & doubt, dread about the Final Judgment.

It just seems to me like Christians might be—no offense, but—a little paranoid.

I can't tell you how many times I washed my hands.
I can't tell you how many times I kneeled down, determined to count my blessings.
The problem of prayer & how not to get distracted . . .

Dear God. Stop. I wish there was some way I could be sure you were getting your mail. Stop. If I didn't really believe in you, why would I be so frightened of being left behind? Stop. I must have faith, right? It's just that one day—I don't know how—I opened my eyes & looked around & didn't trust anyone anymore. Kristin Arlington says I'm a conspiracy theorist. Stop. I do read a lot of detective stories. Stop. Are you mad, God? I want to try to keep believing. I really do. Stop. Whatever you do, I don't want to be smote down.

Define as: *inflict a heavy blow on, with a hand, tool, or weapon*

Define as: *affect suddenly with deep feeling, such as love or infatuation*

Point of interest: to be smitten & to be smote come from the same source

Kristin simplifies: *Love is pain.*

Confirmation Class, St. Paul's of Shorewood Lutheran, 1990.

I am ten years old, year of first doubt & first palpable longing. Pastor Lee says: *The sacred character of the number ten is used in apocalyptic symbolism.*

New Math:

3   (Biblical number for completion, as in *Trinity*)

+ 7   (Biblical number for completion, as in *Creation*)

———

10   (Biblical number for ultimate completion, as in *God's almighty power*)

See, see, my playmate, come out & play with me
And bring your dollies three
Climb up my apple tree

How do we know when the time comes to "put away childish things"?

Paul & the Corinthians had been on my mind. As had the Fruits of the Spirit. I was good at memorizing my catechism, but more & more the stories felt like fiction.

Holler down my rain barrel, slide through my cellar door
And we'll be jolly friends, forever evermore

"The End Times are coming," Kristin warned.

There's a word for this, too. *Caveat.*

Define as: *Latin for "beware"*

Define as: *form of a contract clause that stipulates a particular requirement*

"We have to save the people who haven't been saved—or their blood will be on our hands."

Reading List:

- *Nancy Drew, The Secret of the Old Clock* by Carolyn Keene
- *Holy Bible, New International Version* by God & Others
- *Hardy Boys Mystery Series* by Franklin W. Dixon
- *Luther's Small Catechism* by Martin Luther (with Divine Inspiration)

The First Commandment: You must have no other gods.

Q: What does this mean?
A: We must fear, love, & trust God more than anything.

Dear God, I fear you more than anything, but I'm having trouble with the other two. Don't smote, please.

Jump rope. Double Dutch. Tetherball. Hopscotch. Reading rocket. Name on board. Punishment: clean rabbit cage. One check after my name for talking. Check plus on "guide words" assignment. *God sees everything.* Must earn a plus on multiplication tables. *A pleasure to have in class.* Kickball. Better than the boys. Empty out lunchbox before bringing home. Practice scales, chords, arpeggios. Save Joy from eternal damnation. Knitting at Pioneer Girls. So-so.

Introduction to the Scientific Method, West Seattle Christian School, 1990.

I am ten years old & smitten with the notion of proof.
Kristin says, "You don't need proof if you have faith."
I want to know—*what could it hurt?*

Mrs. Rice writes with pink chalk: *All empirical tests begin with accepting or rejecting the null hypothesis.*

Tetherball tournament. Foursquare. Reading rocket (second time this week!). No name on board. Plus for "citizenship." *God is always watching.* Even in the bathroom? That doesn't seem right. Umbrella turned inside out in windstorm. Mom will be mad. Low score on penmanship again, but high in phonics. Study new vocab words. Save Joy from eternal damnation. Help more at home with the dishes.

Vocabulary List:

- Arbitrary
- Paucity
- Status quo

"Dad, I think I might be going to hell."
   (My mother is out with friends, playing Bingo. We are home eating popcorn, watching *James Bond*.)

   "Nonsense! What's this all about?"

"It's just a feeling I have. I'm afraid to go to sleep at night."

"But you know Jesus Christ is your Lord & Savior. You should take great comfort in that."

"Only . . . *how* do I know?"

"You know how you know! It's the *truth*."
   (Taking his glasses off now, lurching forward as if on a train.)

"I'm afraid when the Great Tribulation comes, I'll wake up, & everyone else will be gone."

"It's a simple equation," my father decreed: "Believe & you live—end of story."

FAITH = LIFE (eternal)

DOUBT = DEATH (eternal)

My hands were very cold. I had a Spy Tech magnifying glass, a periscope, & a fingerprint kit. Any number multiplied times zero became a zero itself. It was hard to tell the difference between *shrinking* & *expanding*, though they were polar opposites. Kristin's mother had two miscarriages in a row. After that, she had five kids, all healthy. Kristin was the oldest. She was pronounced a prodigy.

   Define as: *an unusually gifted or intelligent young person*

         Define as: *an omen or spontaneous manifestation of divine will*

Point of interest: *a child who—by the age of ten—has mastered one of more skills generally undertaken only by adults*

Ten was the cut-off, so I understood then, with some disappointment & some relief, that I wasn't destined to be a prodigy: not in math or music or even in chess, which I was only beginning to learn.

"Why are they called knights when they're really horses?"

"It doesn't matter what they're called; it's what they *do* that's important."
(Kristin had long, straight, yellow hair & muscles in her legs like ropes.)

"Tell me again about the Four Horsemen of the Apocalypse. I'm scared of them, but I think I want to know."

"*War, Famine, Pestilence, Death.* They represent the plagues we'll have to face in the End Times."

"Real or metaphorical?"

"Both, I suppose."

"What about Purgatory?"

(Shaking her head.) "We don't believe in that."

"Why not?"

"Because it's antiquated—& it's also Roman Catholic."

"So are the Catholics going to hell?" (barefoot on my bed with a magnetic chess set: *stalling*)

"It's unclear from the Scriptures, but my father says it doesn't look good."

The null hypothesis is the prediction that an observed difference is due to chance alone & not the result of systemic cause

In other words, she wrote: THERE IS NO SIGNIFICANCE

At Joy's house, her mother did nude yoga in the living room, stretched backwards across a balance ball. They kept pictures from when Joy & Rafael were born—each bloody head emerging from the dark delta of hair. *Are you grossed out?* she asked. *Don't worry. I was too at first, but it's only natural. My mom says people shouldn't be afraid of their bodies.* We ate Grape-Nuts and drank goat's milk & leapt up & down on an enormous trampoline. *Are there any new capers to investigate? Erna Hunt's recycle can has a dozen empty bottles. All vodka, I think, but there could be some whiskey, too.*

"You're really not worried about the end of the world?"

"Scare tactic," she sighed, somersaulting.

Suddenly desperate & fearing tears—"Can I become a Jew?"

"I'm not sure. I think it's one of those things: you either are or you aren't.   Sorry."

There's a word for this, too. *Dualism.*

Define as: *the perspective that the universe is discretely arranged as a series of binary oppositions*

Mind *or* Body Good *or* Evil Male *or* Female Heaven *or* Hell Temporal *or* Eternal Jew *or* Gentile

Say, say, my playmate, don't come & play with me
Don't bring your dollies three
Cut down my apple tree

Lying in the grass afterward, cloud-gazing:

"Did you know a girl is born with all the eggs she'll ever have?"

"But that doesn't make sense, does it? Why do people go around saying *Don't put all your eggs in one basket* if all your eggs already are?"

Shrugs: "My mom can't have any more babies."

"Neither can mine."

"She says she likes the sexual freedom."

"Oh . . . I don't think my mother feels free."

"I wonder when I'll get my period. We're going to have a menarche party, & I'll get a new dress & a fertility goddess."

Jealous: "Is that a Jewish thing?"

"No. It's pagan. We're more spiritual than orthodox anyway."

"I want to get mine in the bathtub, so it won't make a mess, & I won't have to tell anyone."

"But you'll tell me, right? And Kristin?"

"You maybe. Kristin's too prissy about things like that."

"Isn't it strange how once we start bleeding, it's the beginning of the end of our eggs?"

Fall off my rainbow into my cellar door
And we'll be enemies, forever evermore

I was so tired. Every time I closed my eyes I thought of Armageddon: how death was waiting for me, how God was looking on, displeased. Hell-fires. Indentured servitude to Satan. *We can't prove the Bible true, & we can't prove the Bible untrue.* Gold stars on all my catechism quizzes. *It's a matter of faith. Men you can fool, but God sees what's in your heart.* There were other things, too. Like how Kristin Arlington said she was more like Nancy Drew than I was. "Joy can be Bess, she's *always* been Bess, but you're more George than Nancy. Think about what we know: Nancy Drew has blond hair, like I do. George is tall & wiry with short dark hair, like you." George was the tomboy. I didn't want to be the tomboy. It was *my* mystery club. It was *my* idea. *All great persons of faith pass through difficult periods of doubt. They often experience these periods as God testing them.* Would I "pass"? Would I be confirmed a Christian or a liar? I read the Bible. (Psalms, Beatitudes.) I tried to pray. But it was Purgatory: here on Earth, already.

Sayings:

- *An apple a day keeps the doctor away*

I ate the red flesh only & threw the core away. Sometimes I gave the apple to my teacher.

- *The apple has been implicated as an original fruit of the Fall*

P·R·E·L·A·P·S·A·R·I·A·N

- *To add or subtract fractions, you must first make a common denominator*

How was this possible? Even the same age, we wore our numbers differently, my ten & her ten & hers . . .

- *First law of thermodynamics: Energy can be neither created nor destroyed; it can only change forms*

I wanted to be all soul & no body. *All or nothing.* Could someone please siphon me free as if through a crazy straw?

- *A mathematical notation indicating the number of times a quantity is multiplied by itself; the power to which a number is raised*

E·X·P·O·N·E·N·T

- *"Checkmate" is when someone wins & someone loses; "stalemate" is when two opponents reach an impasse*

I don't like "rooks." I like "castles." They look like castles to me, so that's what I'm going to call them.

- *We will make piñatas for Cinco de Mayo, & the process we will use is called papier-mâché*

The candy I wouldn't touch, the sticky paper—my nascent fist splitting the donkey's purple body

("Guess you didn't know your own strength," she smiled as we stood together
in the Tootsie Roll rain.)

See you later, Alligator.
After awhile, Crocodile.

After school, running all the way there: "I have to know—what about that box in your basement?"

"You have to be quiet," Kristin shushed, stowing me away in her bedroom. "My parents are doing the Lord's work."

"What does that mean?"

Indignant: "It's Tuesday at 4:00. They're *procreating*."

"Don't they have enough kids? And you said yourself they hate Catholics."

"Not *hate*. We don't *hate* anyone. But the Bible does say, *Go forth & multiply*."

"So the box. Tell me. It's important."

Sitting down at her desk, matter-of-factly: "Water, granola, medical supplies. My mom bought it for"—hesitating—"those not delivered in the Rapture."

It was as I feared. Mrs. Arlington had prepared the equivalent of an earthquake kit with only me in mind, knowing I was destined to be the last child left behind in our neighborhood: orphaned daughter of my God-fearing parents, my God-loving grandmother . . . Why had I even bothered going to Bible School? When the End Times came, everyone would see what a sham I was, what a sinner . . . And singing in the choir, & high marks in catechism class . . . what about *cataclysm* class? That was my unhappy kismet . . . My own mother having forecasted this fate: *Julie Marie, you're headed for a fall!*

Dear God. Stop. I guess I should have realized by now there is no "stalemate" where faith is concerned. There are winners & losers, like with everything else. Stop. The winners are called "saved" & the losers are called "damned," & I don't think anybody in my family ever figured I would be one of the damned. Prodigal maybe, but where's my fatted calf? Stop. I'm being what my mother calls "flip," & it's very disrespectful. God, how did I end up skating on such thin ice? I was guarding my king so closely, I thought. Stop. Now I'm mixing metaphors. It's dreadful. I'll never be a writer, but with the End Times coming, I probably won't ever be an adult, so what does it matter? Stop. Only, it does matter. God, I want to grow up. Otherwise, what was the point of all this travail? Stop. I'm not sure, though. I might be lying to you right now, which doesn't bode well for me, but since I'm already in danger of seven years of beef jerky & dehydrated vegetables—I guess I can say anything. Stop. I'm not sure I want to grow up either. Maybe I'm "bringing this all on myself": something else my mother likes to say. I got my first training bra & thought I should be happy, thought it's what I wanted, but then I put it on & it made me sick to my stomach & it made my skin crawl, & I had to pull it off as quickly as possible & cut it up with scissors & throw it away. Stop. Like I said, I was guarding my king. I thought I knew where all the pieces were. But now I'm in "check," & I can't get out of it, & I wish there was some way I could just disappear— "abdicate," I suppose, would be the proper term. Just die now & save you all the trouble. Stop. Or be absolved, once & for all, of everything. Put away childish things for good.

There's a word for this, too. *Capitulation.*

Define as: *a document containing the terms of surrender*

Define as: *enumeration of the main parts of a subject*

Mrs. Rice was the principal of our elementary school. She taught science classes & emphasized the value of empirical study. *Trust your experience! It is the ultimate educator.* I liked her because she had a gold tooth & wide hips & warm hands & a daughter named Ginger who had red hair & freckles & flew airplanes for a living. Kristin Arlington's father was a pilot, but I never knew until Ginger that women were eligible.

Special Terms:

- Falsifiability
- Contingency
- Defeasibility

Karl Popper helped us understand that no empirical hypothesis, proposition, or theory can be considered "scientific" if it does not admit the possibility of a contrary case.

Contrary Cases:

- It is possible (though doubtful) that Kristin Arlington may make a better Nancy Drew
- It is possible that when we pray we are only speaking to air
- It is possible (though doubtful) that someone may find my body beautiful
- It is possible that nothing extraordinary happens when we die
- It is possible (though doubtful) that I may survive the End Times

A sailor went to sea sea sea
To see what he could see see see
But all that he could see see see
Was the bottom of the deep blue sea sea sea

When she spoke of Zeno & his Paradoxes, I knew at once I was in over my head.

Zeno's arguments are among the first examples of a method called—the pink chalk again, for emphasis—
REDUCTIO AD ABSURDUM, *or proof by contradiction*

Joy, smacking her gum & filling out flashcards:

Belief in plurality is misguided
Belief in motion is misguided
Belief in change is misguided

TO DO:

- Run 30 laps at Denny Middle School track
- Swim 400 Freestyle x 400 Breaststroke x 400 Backstroke x 400 Butterfly
- Abdominal crunches first thing every morning: 500-1000, depending on time
- Repeat abdominal crunches before bed (double morning amount)
- No sweets, no meats, no grains, no starchy vegetables, no exceptions!

"Mom, how do I know if I'm saved?"
(We are standing in the kitchen, knives in our hands . . .)

"What do you mean *how do you know?* You've read the catechism. You know the rules."

"But I mean *really*. If the world ended tomorrow, where would I be?"
     (Arranging the table: spoons & forks & plates & glasses . . .)

"Why dwell on that now? Why be difficult?"

"It's not dwelling so much as wondering—but also *really needing to know.*
     (How we cling to this ritual: safety of fixed places around an infinite circle . . .)

"The Bible's the best way to live. It's the safest. Your father was the one who saved me."

"And you just—*converted*? Just like that. Snap of your fingers, & you suddenly believed in God?"
     (We are standing in the kitchen, knives in our hands . . .)

"Think of it as an insurance policy. Think of it as a safety net, just in case you fall."

                    But aren't we fallen already? Isn't that the problem?

"So are you saying you don't really believe? That you don't really *have* to?
     (Opening & closing the microwave door: this ritual also: this old, familiar heat . . .)

"I'm saying: *Better safe than sorry.* I'm saying: *Proceed as if it were true.*"

There's a word for this, too. *Verisimilitude.*

     Define as: *appearance of truth; approximation of reality*

               Define as: *artifice or illusion; a surrogate for truth in the absence of its confirmation*

"Mom, do you think there is such a thing as a *true believer*?"

Affirmation of Baptism Ceremony, Calvary Lutheran Church, 1992.

There we were:

this gaggle of girls—

row of goose eggs in our white gowns

(boys among us draped in sackcloth brown)

Swift Achilles, who couldn't catch up . . .

The Message in the Hollow Oak, The Mystery of the Ivory Charm, The Clue in the Jewel Box

Hole/Whole   Hollow/Hallow

The Quest of the Missing Map, The Hidden Window Mystery, The Invisible Intruder, The Thirteenth Pearl

Slow tortoise, who couldn't be surpassed . . .

Questions:

- *Will the supplicants please rise?*
- *Will the pint of wine turn me tipsy?*
- *Will the wafer expand my waistline?*

- *Will the supplicants please repeat after me?*
- *Will it hurt?*
- *Will it stop on a dime?*

- *Will the supplicants please kneel?*
- *Will it come before (lead)?*
- *Will it come after (follow)?*

- *Will the supplicants please repeat after me?*
- *Will it leave marks?*
- *Will it make change?*

I now pronounce you *nevermore & nevermore* the sweet heat of summer (short-lived) & the raven at the window & the "Fall of the House of Usher" & yellow hair & Ned Nickerson's red roadster with old-fashioned running boards & *felix culpa* & the fourth state of matter & *mea culpa* & doubt ubiquitous as donut holes at Sunday morning coffee hour & stalling & stalling & the missing rib of Adam (& the missing rib of Cher) & God calling with no one to answer & Jane Eyre's antidote—"I must keep in good health, & not die"—& *cardinal numbers* & *ordinal numbers* & *last star to the right & on till morning* & manna from heaven & MENSA on earth & *imaginary numbers* & more clues than could ever add up.

Epilogue (or) Epiphany:

"What do you think the last word is?"

(*A beat.*) (Not looking up.) (Not even blinking.)

"*Rip*—as in Rip Van Winkle."

NEXT

This circle drawn in sand:

This halo of string spread across the living room floor:

Marbles—did you bring yours?
Bright collection of agate balls
Put 'em in then, let 'em go
Keepsies or *quitsies*—you choose

I have contributed 3 marbles: lapis we will call *how* topaz we will call *if* quartz-stone we will call *why*

He has contributed 3 also: turquoise we will call *then* onyx we will call *though* moon-stone we will call *yet*

The shooter is *Next*.

Surely you remember the objective of this game:

exclusion—

eviction from that favored sphere
(inclusion in exchange for . . .)

Remember, not all can be chosen—in a church whisper, from one who believed herself CHOSEN

(. . . exile)

"Losing your marbles," see, is more than just losing your mind. It's losing your place at the common table. It's losing your place in line. It's disappearing—receding—right before your own marble-gemstone eyes.

(The shooter is *Next*.) (The marbles are captured.)
(Words are ransomed, letter by letter.)

The woman at the bagel shop has seen me around. I come in every Thursday for the paper. Order my coffee in a traveler's cup, even though I almost always stay. Take a whole booth for just myself & my bag. Sometimes wear headphones, sometimes not. Laugh aloud reading syndicated "Savage Love."

I have seen her around: the woman at the bagel shop—with her blunt-cut hair, dark & thick & smooth as pitch; her flawless, Dionysian complexion. How I have studied her: easy movement through a world of strangers (who address her by name (draw up chairs at her table (stop to coo at the baby who lulls to sleep in her arms.

yet, how, why, if, then, now

The shooter is *Next*.

(Something about proximity, about ambit.
        (Something about parity, about difference.

Do I stand accountable for all the blood intentionally shed? For the body, like the circle, left unbroken?

Think of the women who can't conceive—but yearn to:

Think of the women who could conceive—but choose not to:

(Think of my place at their table)

Nye writes—"It's late, but everything comes next."

how late?
why everything?

Bodies like continents, severed before birth.

(Something called callowness, called merit.
   (Something called secession, called union.

(progression in time or space)

NO VACANCY
NO AGENCY
PARTIAL ADJACENCY

Boy Next Door & Girl Next Door so conveniently located they need not re-route

PANGAEA ULTIMA

TENON   &   MORTISE

DOVETAIL, STORK, SWAN

Have you read the fine print?
    Have you balanced the Future's checkbook, paid out in small debts to the Past?

why, if, yet, then, how, now

    Who will take care of you when you're old?
    Isn't that what children are for?
Surely by now we have staked a better reason.

                                    Small plug for posterity:

                        Twinkle, twinkle, little star,
                            Don't you worry where you are;
                    When you're old & when you're gray,
                        I will light your wizened way.

    Keepsies or quitsies:

                                    The shooter is *Next.*

First comes love, next comes marriage, next comes the baby in the baby carriage

"I'm scared. Are you?"—in a tree-house, if we had one, gazing up at the stars

"Not *orphans* exactly. Never *widows*."

(What to make of our inexpressible fate.)

The new word on the next generation is that we should wait:

> something about abstinence, about estrangement:
> something called surrender, called asylum.

The new stone on the old path is that we should want:

> to buy into the next line of human stock:
> build collateral at least, boost morale.

I see her everywhere: the woman from the bagel shop. We could not have planned it. In the supermarket: her basket filled with Gerber's strained peas & rack of lamb. Spare ribs, Dijon mustard. French-cut greens & Vlasic dills & bread crumbs destined for eggplant parmesan. I get hungry just grazing her cart.

It's early yet, & everything's still next:

> heaping plates & second helpings:

> expensive *boulders* that gleam inside the ring

"You could turn this all around," my mother writes. "You could put this all behind you."

> *yet, if, then, how, why, now*

(Something about sanctity—or common sense.
  (Something about dignity—or danger.

> "What will become of you," she mourns, "all alone in your empty life?"

But for now, there remains this hypothesis called Next Time. Next man in the grocery store line who scans my hand for a wedding band. Next man who dramatically holds the door. Next offer to take the seat beside him. The muscle-flex, the skin-caress. *Jesus, I thought you girls were sisters!*

Hole in my heart like a shunted thing, like a creature that clings. (Sessile.) (Infantile.)

(progression in space or time)

Have you read the fine print?
      Have you misunderstood the requirements?
    From whence does your confusion spring?

                                    The shooter is *Next.*

"I didn't make the rules—God did."

"The stork is a symbol for happiness. Shouldn't that tell us something?"

"Your name won't pass on as the only girl, but what about your genes, your bloodline?"

"She can never give you what a man can."

"For Christ's sake, couldn't you just pretend?"

It frightens me to think how angry I am. *What's next?* Is this the wit's end, the proverbial straw & the invalid camel? Someone loses, & someone wins? (Tiddlywinks, Parcheesi.) A new restaurant in a different neighborhood. The same woman sits happily ensconced with friends. (Battleship.) Square table: north, south, east, west. They each know the direction they're coming from, proceed like clockwork. Mile-high salads with melba toast. Watching cholesterol & waistlines. (Connect Four.) Wife / Mother. Diamond / Diaper Bag. (Tic Tac Toe.) XOXO. The platitudes we're supposed to recite. The sacrifices we're supposed to enjoy. *But what if they're true? What if you've always wanted the life you were supposed to want?* (RACK-O!) All your ducks in a row, all your cards lined up in perfect chronological order. *I mean, frankly, I can't quite imagine the alternative.* (UNO?) And how to respond without seeming defensive . . . How not to lash through the forms . . . SINGLE MARRIED DIVORCED WIDOWED. Where is my (LIFE) here? Where is my NONE OF THE ABOVE?

now, then, why, if, yet, how

At home, in our old house, which we rent for a song; which swelters through the summers & shivers through the winters; which grows morning glories & tiger lilies wild; which holds a porch swing & a piece of very old, oddly beautiful stained glass, an eve's worth of hornets' nests—

My Love teaches me the wonder of natural language searching

We have just switched from dial-up to DSL
We have just switched from Google to Ask.com

(progression through time & space)

"For this kind of search, questions are phrased in a familiar way; keywords are factored out for answers. Nesting is no longer required."

(Love) & (Marriage) & (Baby Carriage)

Is it possible to undo the old linkages, reset our passwords, arrange for different default modes?

(SIMPLER) & (TIME)
(ABSOLUTE) & (TRUTH)

Or that word I like, from a class you took, that I walked around muttering for days:

DISAMBIGUATION:

(From many possible translations, selecting the one with minimum semantic distance)

OR   *(Determining which of several alternatives was selected by the user)*   OR

(Clarification that follows from the dispersal of ambiguity)

I pass the woman in her neighborhood. I have never seen her in mine. I walk two miles or stand on a city bus to buy coffee & a bagel at her doorstep. We exchange no animosity, neither any greeting. We suffer from a mild case of faint recognition & understand implicitly in the passing that our lives play out parallel to one another: proximal without intersecting, perpetually adjacent. *Next.* In the post office, our letters lay atop each other, ink smearing her monogrammed crest, my incidental flap. Her Sabbath & my aimless stroll through Squirrel Hill & onward into Oakland. She behind the wheel of her dual-airbag, eight-passenger minivan & I—pedestrian—scurrying across her path & into her periphery, where perennially & indeterminately I reside. In the bank, our transaction slips lay atop each other, ink smearing her deposit, my withdrawal. Her Much to my Little. Her "valued customer since 1986" to my "not even born till 1979."

It's early in the game still, but late in the round.
I lug trash to the alley, disambiguate the lilacs.

What my father used to say, when we were still talking: "Don't you worry your pretty little head about it."

What my Bible used to say, when I was still reading: "Consider, ye faithful, the lilies of the field."
What will become of me?   I wonder.

It is not a prayer exactly. It is not even a question for sure.

Perhaps it is a natural language search.

The shooter is *Next.*

(The shooter is Cupid.)
(The shooter is John Hinckley Jr. or John Wilkes Booth
or Lee Harvey Oswald.)
(The story is a history lesson.)
(The artist is Henry Darger.) (The poet is silent.)

("The proof is in the pudding.")
(The garter is white.) (The bouquet is loaded.)
(Lilies make me weep or sneeze.)

Is it customary to feel so alone in the world, so at odds with the ones I once loved?

After all, wasn't it my father who taught me to play marbles?
Wasn't it he who passed on to me this language?

What of heredity?

That is:

Do I stand accountable for all the blood intentionally shed? For the body, like the circle, left unbroken?

Inside, it is roughly a hundred degrees. My Love reads by the fan, eating ice cubes. In a large, stylish house with central heating & air, the woman from the bagel shop is also—may be also—eating ice cubes. She wears a sweater even, because the house is so cool, & feels herself pulled in a hundred tedious directions while her husband travels across the state on business.

(progression through space & time)

Red Rover, Red Rover, Send Someone Right Over.
There will be someone watching over when she dies.

It comes: cold fact on a hot day, standing in the alley in a bee-storm.
You have nothing to show for yourself, that familiar buzz.
You don't belong to anything, & nothing belongs to you.
(Not in any way they can recognize. Not in any way the law divines.)

then, if, yet, why, how, now

And I want to say to K. who is married now—whose wedding a year ago I nearly ruined—

"Forgive me, friend."

And to B. also, whose wedding I cannot even bear to attend:

"Forgive me."

And they do, & they have, but things will not be the same between us.

What were we then—place cards for each other at a crowded table?

Bookmarks until a husband turned the page?

What kind of story was it anyway—*once upon a time* & *happy ever after*?

It angers me to think how frightened I am. *What's next?* Erasure? The mighty Pink Pearl & its steady effacement: A., my Love, *my "partner," my "room-mate," my "friend."* I can hear the strangers chatter already: *Such a shame. Sharp girl, not bad-looking—why do you suppose she never found a man?* How will they know? Who will remind them? When the day comes & I can no longer defend myself, my story . . . when I look back & the choices seem so much less my own—diminished by euphemisms, or left all together untold. I take photographs now with my mind, obsessive as a character in a Cameron Crowe film. Polaroids—because they are precise & immediate. The device is called a JoyCam. I write in black fine-tipped pen on each blank-white border: THIS IS REAL, THIS HAPPENED, THIS IS WHO I LOVED, THIS IS WHAT WE DID, THIS IS HOW WE PROGRESSED TOGETHER THROUGH SPACE & TIME

(My First) (My Last) (My Next)

I find compassion now for my father. I choose to remember him as I hope he remembers me: *happy.* I choose to remember us with rug-burned knees, vying for each other's marbles. Of his tape recorder with the tiny microphone, where he asked me to record my child-thoughts. *For posterity,* he said. *For keeps.*

"What kind of day is it, Julie?"

"Pretty—big sun, puffy clouds."

"What's that boat in the harbor called?"

"A *ferry* boat! Like fairies in the woods, but spelled different."

"What's your favorite game to play with your daddy?"

"Marbles!" I cried. "I love marbles!"

Because this is necessary:

Last Will & Testament of _____ *[Testator], resident of* _____ *[City]*

I place my lapis in the circle. *How can anything be simple? How can anything be easy?*

He lends his turquoise to the circle. *Then let go & let God. Then lean not on your own understanding.*

Because we have lived & loved together, & there must be some record of this:

being of sound & disposing mind & memory & over the age of 18 years . . .

I place my topaz in the circle. *If things don't turn out the way we expect . . . If life surprises us with unconventional blessings . . .*

He lends his onyx to the circle. *Though it may seem "right" to you, or "good," or "true," God commands the only Moral Way.*

Because I believe in the tangible & intangible beauty of this humble bequest:

do make, publish, & declare this to be my last & only Will . . .

I place my quartz-stone in the circle. *Why are you afraid of asking questions? Why are you afraid of how I might respond?*

He lends his moon-stone to the circle. *Man is weak, yet God forgives him. The body is weak, yet the soul offers strength.*

Because this is true:

Not being actuated by any duress, menace, fraud, mistake, or undue influence, I offer the following . . .

The shooter is *Next.*

For my father, who asked me to disambiguate love & call it treason

For my mother, who asked me to turn caryatid instead of human being

For this verse, the last of the refuse I thought not to save: how it returns like words in a bottle—

They toil not, neither do they spin. Yet even Solomon in all his splendor was not arrayed like one of these. Not orphans exactly, never widows. Lilacs profuse, spilling over the fence post. Not like a poem exactly. Not quite a sign. My bare feet in the high grass. My bare heart in the warm wind. Walking home again. Up the front steps. Through the front door. All the extraordinary prepositions between (Here Now) & (There Then) & (Somewhere in the Future). All the little joys of conjugation before the last amen. *It's late, but everything comes next.* Honey in your tea. Balsamic vinaigrette on bright green leaves.

SOLSTICE

yet, why, how, now, then, if

"Two ways to look at this, I guess"—in a tree-house, if we had one, gazing up at the stars

"Threshold of the longest, gateway to the shortest."

(What to make of our incalculable days.)

ACKNOWLEDGMENTS

This book was written in Pittsburgh, Pennsylvania, between 2004 & 2006. I wish to thank Amy Patterson, Connie Angermeier, John Miller, & the Department of Social and Decision Sciences at Carnegie Mellon University for their faith in me & for the cherished designation, "Poet Laureate of SDS." I also remain grateful in perpetuity for the mentorship I received from Kathryn Flannery, Lucy Fischer, Lisa Parker, & Katie Hogan during this time.

In addition, I wish to thank Bruce Beasley & James Allen Hall, two poets of immense talent & influence on my writing life. This book would never have been written without the transformative education I received in Bruce Beasley's 2002 experimental poetics class at Western Washington University. And the news of this book's publication could not have arrived under more auspicious circumstances than the day James Allen Hall & I took our living-poet pictures at the *Dead Poets Society* film site in Middletown, Delaware.

Many thanks are due to the kind & diligent staff at A Room of Her Own Foundation & Red Hen Press, & to my long-time poet-hero, C. D. Wright, for selecting this book for the 2014 To the Light-house Prize. I'm still not sure I believe it's true.

Credit is given to Mary Oliver from whose poem "March" the opening epigraph was gratefully borrowed.

"Latchkey" is for Tom Campbell, faithful reader, mentor, & friend. This poem appears in the Fall 2007 issue of *::stonestone::*. "Layover" is for Anna Rhodes, friend at any distance; & for my neighbors, once upon a time, on Plum Way. This poem appears in the Spring 2008 "Genre Blur" issue of *Alligator Juniper*. "Maidenhead" is for David Seal, Suzanne Paola, & Brenda Miller, who have pulled back the fantastical veil. This poem appears in the Spring 2008 ("Violet Issue") of *The Fairy Tale Review*. "Mezzanine" is for Robyn Dawes, Ben Dobyns, & Maureen Seaton: for poignant & particular reasons. "Null" is for Dana Anderson, faithful reader, mentor, & friend. This poem appears in the Fall 2007 issue of *Quarter After Eight*. "Next" is for Angie Griffin: first, last, & always. This poem appears in the Fall 2016 issue of *Bellingham Review*. "Alantic Elegy" is dedicated to C. D. Wright. It was published by the Academy of American Poets Poem-a-Day series on March 28, 2016.

ATLANTIC ELEGY

We see a little farther now and a little farther still
—C.D. Wright

I ask the rain to remit, but not because I am ungrateful
A raincheck for the rain—is such a thing possible?

In Florida, even the cold is warm by comparison
We sit at the ocean's lip as it licks the sand from our toes

Consider instead—the terrifying beauty of alternative

I ask the sun to pumice our faces, blind us humble and good
Incumbent sun, so long accustomed to winning the stars' wars

Consider although—like trying to whistle with a mouth full of Saltines

We only know what we know
We only see what we see

I ask the space to persist after the hyphen that separates
Birth from death, to leave the parenthesis like a gap tooth

Then to no one in particular, I say, *What age is not a tender age?*

This hapless haptic misses her Blackberry
Such tender buttons, were they not?
The tiny Underwood slick inside her pocket

I ask the lifeguard not to hang the purple flag
For jellyfish and sting rays and the floating terror

Imagine if that were your name!

Also answers to: *bluebottle, Physalia physalis, man-of-war*

Consider except—Luminara of a word—bag of sand with a light inside
Synonym for human perhaps?

I am not opposed to the idea of being lost—
like the red balloon, Mylar with a silver underside—
buoyed along these stubby waves

Consider forever—which is a trick command

A seagull tugs the string of the beached balloon
You see it more clearly now: a webbed design, the visage of Spiderman

When the rain comes, it is warm kisses, little white beads

Grown-ups stick their tongues out like children do

It's not over till it's over—and then, too soon

BIOGRAPHICAL NOTE

Julie Marie Wade is the author of four collections of poetry, including *When I Was Straight* (A Midsummer Night's Press, 2014) and *Postage Due* (White Pine Press, 2010), and four collections of lyric nonfiction, including *Catechism: A Love Story* (Noctuary Press, 2016) and *Wishbone: A Memoir in Fractures* (Bywater Books, 2014; Colgate University Press, 2010). She has received an Al Smith Individual Artist Fellowship from the Kentucky Arts Council, a grant from the Barbara Deming Memorial Fund, and the Lambda Literary Award for Lesbian Memoir. She teaches in the creative writing program at Florida International University in Miami.

CPSIA information can be obtained at www.ICGtesting.com
Printed in the USA
BVOW04n1557080916

461034BV00004B/26/P